WALKIN' THE MAT

PAST IMPRESSIONS OF ABERDEEN

compiled by

RON WINRAM F.S.A. (Scot.) and **ANDREW CLUER** A.L.A.

Dedicated to
Margaret and Brenda

D1610761

CONTENTS

INTRODUCTION

The title *Aberdeen: Walkin' The Mat* takes in snippets of information from all walks of life along the way; necessarily episodic in nature which epitomises the city's character.

The city has always held its own against all comers. There is no need to boost up its beauties; yet Aberdonians have a penchant for obscure places (the byeways). Information concerning the street names and their associations is therefore the basis for this 'Unofficial Guide' compiled by Andrew Cluer and Ron Winram through pre-war Aberdeen. It is the amalgamation of little and great places in book form.

 The men who 'made' Aberdeen

1

THE OLD HIGHWAY INTO ABERDEEN

'The Dee is a beautiful river', said Lord Byron. It still is 'the rivergate' to Aberdeen, though Thomas The Rhymer, the 'Inverury Soothsayer', predicted that 'Dee and Don will run in one'. Both rivers have been linked, now that the Ring Road Anderson Drive has reached Persley. Another school of thought saw the prophecy being fulfilled when the universities amalgamated in 1860. A poem published in *Alma Mater* (1912) underlines the fact that the universities supplied scholarships for the academics of Deeside and Donside; it poses the question, 'whar wid the warld an' cities be, but for the men of Don and Dee? . . .

The approach road to Aberdeen was obscure until the nineteenth-century improvements. It was not without hazards, as the stretch of shingle upstream from Mill o' Leggart was haunted by the 'Green Lady'. Water kelpies were last seen there in the 1830s. Their dark countenance and shining eyes are not forgotten when there is a drowning. Those choosing to use The Foords o' Dee were in addition endangered by logs floating down from mountain forests to the Pierhead. Sometimes these were buried in shingle to prevent salmon nets being torn.

> Folk then turned out the coach to see
> heard her horn at the Brig o' Dee,
> the soun' young and auld gart rin
> to see the mail come dashin' in.
> (James Smith, 1830)

The Brig o' Dee, and in the distance the old cottages of Ruthrieston and Foords o' Dee. Cartloads of hay or peat from nearby mosses that travelled this way were weighed at the steelyard at the Bridge-head.

There was a wifie sat on the brig o' Dee
An' aye she cried 'Gie me! Gie me!'
An' there was another wifie
An' she aye took what she had
An' sae she niver wintet.
Which o' thae wifies wad ye be?

Willie Buck had a coo,
her name was Billy Binty
she loupit ower the Brig o' Dee,
like ony cove o' ninty.

The last line refers to a corruption of Covenanter and said to refer to the capture of Aberdeen by Montrose in 1639.

Old rhyme concerning drownings and kelpies,
Bloodthirsty Dee
She needs three,
But bonny Don,
She needs none.

> There wis a maid in Bervie
> and she longed for a baby;
> she took her father's greyhound
> and rolled it in a plaidie
> singing hish a bishy, bow wow
> lang leggies now now,
> an' twerena for your grey beardie
> I wad kiss you now, now . . .

Carriages, including the old four-in-hand or the Royal Mail, after crossing the narrow arches of the Brig o' Dee, turned at a sharp angle towards the city and the Hardgate, the road surface becoming 'mean, filthy and dubby'. After the Packhorse Bridge beside Ruthrieston Market stance was past; progressing townward towards Castle Street, the wheels splashed through the Howeburn, near where that stream powered the Upper and Lower Justice Mills. The 'traces' had to be deftly handled along Langstane Place down the break-neck Windmill Brae, then across the Bow Brig to the Green; turning right across the Mautmill Burn via 'the briggie', the coachman took the streaming horses along Fisher Row, clattering over the cassies of St. Katherine's Hill whilst ascending the Shiprow. Finally, the New Inn at Castle Street was approached via Exchequer Row.

Hardgate remained the ceremonial street of Aberdeen, even when the pageant of the Riding of the Marches was revived. The first March Stone is at 81 Hardgate and reads, 'I Aberdeen City Royalty'.

An extract from *The Riding of The Marches* (4 September 1889) reads, 'From thence the party went; Their progress still being watched by large numbers of the public. Ascending the steep brae at Willowbank, the rate of speed had to be made very easy, but on reaching the top of the hill, the leaders dashed off at a merry pace, and as the outskirts of the city were traversed, the numbers of spectators became less and less, more scope was afforded for the many varied displays of horsemanship on the part of the Marshalls and Bannermen.'

🐦 The old Packhorse Brig on the approach road from the south.

Salmon fishers from Loch Maree 'bade in the Bothy at The Brig o' Dee'.

Hardgate looking north from 'Dyer's Hall Lane corner.' The latter was widened and became known as Willowbank Road.

THE GATES OF ABERDEEN

The Hardgate and The Windmill Brae,
The Shiprow and The Green,
were then the only thoroughfares
that led to Aberdeen.

William Anderson

History is embedded in street names, and Aberdeen's own street lore is alive.

An Aberdeen street song:
A penny o' chips tae grease my lips;
one, two, three.

THE BROADGATE
From Union Street to Gallowgate

Broad Street was formerly a shopping street that catered for Marischal College's needs. Wooden cassies were laid rather than the familiar granite setts so that the sound of clattering hand barrows and hurlies would not interrupt lectures.

Dr William Guild, in a Deed of Mortification dated 1633 gave the senate a house that could be taken down to give the College a more suitable entrance.

Thirty shilling serge suits hung outside the outfitters at College Gate.

Tailors' labels were prestigious in those days, but a knowledge of mottoes was a sure sign of wisdom. Marischal College's motto still encourages intellectual good manners. Lewis Smith (1804–80), the blunt Broad Street bookseller and publisher was kept busy with orders and repartees. When asked if he expected a book on order to arrive soon he retorted: 'Do I command the wind and the waves? . . . It's coming on the steamer.' He spoke too soon, for the 'winds of change' have been blowing in this locality since the turn of our century, when Greyfriars, the only pre-reformation kirk to have survived in the city was removed from the quadrangle of Marischal College. Backing on to it was the Waterhouse, (a reservoir of 1766), and Byron's Lodging which housed the above-named bookshop. Most of the ancient buildings were constructed of Loanhead 'granite', including the *Evening Express* premises which were finally removed for the Town House extension in 1973.

The Wall Street crash dashed the prospects of there being a city square opposite the flamboyant façade. Seabury Cathedral in the English Gothic style in granite by Aberdonian Sir Ninian Comper never materialised due to the Wall Street crash. Its spire, based on that of St. Nicholas Kirk which was destroyed by fire in 1874 was to have soared above the Mitchell Tower. An alternative 'shrine' to local government arose from the intended spot at a later date; its name is St. Nicholas House.

The north side of the Broadgate. 🖝 'Byron's Lodging' is in the foreground and further down the street, the Water-House and fire-station of 1766 which was formerly manned by the shore porters. The new street-line can be seen behind the houses as indicated by the 'frostit' pinnacles of the south front.

🖝 The south side of the Broadgate; Blairton Lane and Raggs Lane led through to the Guestrow.

7

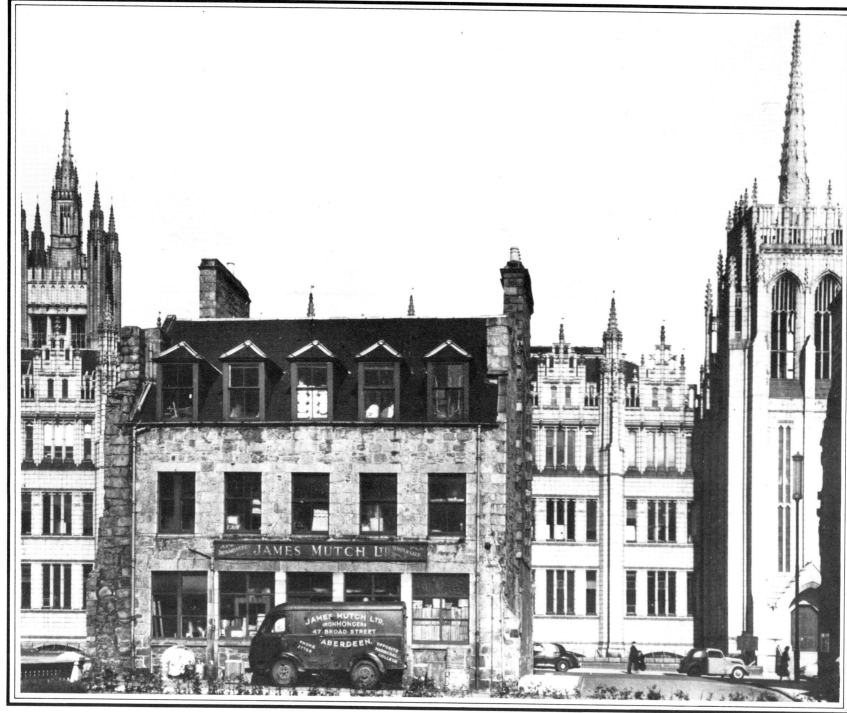

The bowed condition of the leerie was acquired by his sliding down the ladder to save time. Ostlers, and men much accustomed to horseback became bow-legged. Household lighting necessities were 'cannles' oil 'cruisies', 'flint & flourish' or 'tinder box'. Matches were known as 'spunks', 'lucifers' and 'wax vestas'.

The lamps were lit from August to May, street corner lamps for the duration of the summer too. They received a weekly clean with whitening.

We came noo tae The Market Cross,
It stood then anent The Town House,
a structure baith for show and use.
The head post office it was made,
the letters took for folk in trade;
the arches o' it were boarded ower,
A' but ane left, that wis the door.
A man sat in't a' day steady,
letters to tak' and gie ready.
There wisna mony letters then,
jist a few amangst tradin' men;
the cost of postage made them few—
fourpence each office they came through.

(James Smith, 1830)

Dawvid Glibtongue's Harangue

For honest workmen, sharp and keen,
I rede you gang to Aberdeen.
Our sons are famed for manly graces,
our daughters too for dandie dresses;
our local buiks for charmin' readin',
our farmers, bricks for cattle breedin'.
for a' that's noble, grand and jeety,
I point you to 'The Granite City',
We're famed for a' that's great an' gweed,
aye, e'en for makin' potted heid.
In ither cities I hae seen
'fine potted heid fae Aberdeen'.

(James Ogg)

This informal vista of wedding-cake architecture has a stage set quality about it; a production entitled "Mutch" ado about nothing . . . '.

Leerie leerie licht the lamps
lang legs and crookit shanks.
Tak' a stick an' brak' his back,
an' throw him o'er The Broadgate.

CASTLEGATE
From Union Street to Justice Street

Castlegate was the hub of Aberdeen; a meeting place teeming with vitality, just as much as 'The Mat' in Union Street. 'The Rug' lead from Castlegate open market ('The Castler') up Union Street to The Mat, and on Saturday nights it was the custom 'to hae a dander tae the market and hae a rake aroun''. By ten o'clock it was time for The Salvation Army to commence 'beating the drum and saving the souls'.

The names of showmen such as 'Brongo' the public dentist and Danta the herbalist were household names.

The last authentic Timmer Market was held here in its original stance in August 1934, when most of the wares on sale were wooden. Housewives could stock up with items essential for the traditional northeast kitchen such as brose bowls, spurtles, rolling pins, buckets and tubs.

The Feeing Market was another date in the calender of farm servants known as 'halflins'. In the old days recruiting sergeants were on the look out for 'country geordies' and 'toonsers' who wanted to see the world with the army. Today, the name Castlegate stands fairly and squarely for 'Heritage'. Its chief glories, the old characters are away, and the distinctive smell it had, not unlike the original New Market.

When Saturday nicht-caps his pate,
An' fowks are oot their erran's
Oor broad, capacious Castlegate
Presents a thrang appearance
There's fiddlers, preachers, bargain jacks,
An' medical pretenders,
An' maids wi' creels, an' men wi' packs
An' fruit an' sweetie vendors

Market cries of the Castlegate:
'Hard corns, soft corns, black corns, seedy corns; I cure them all.'

'Bananas all the way from the Canary Islands; bloody oranges from the Holy Land.'

Chippit fruit, bargain bags of cheese cuttings and cold meat cuttings all helped folk to feed large families.

'All aboard for the Bathing Station and The Beach.' A waggonette plied between Castle Street and the sea beach. In the background is the Salvation Army Citadel, (1896) by James Souttar, who travelled the Continent looking for architectural inspiration during the time that Ludwig of Bavaria was building his castles. Nevertheless there is a northeast saying, 'brose-fed, but castle-minded'.

The Yule Eve Sang

Rise up guid wife an' be nae sweir
tae deal wi' yer breid as lang's yer here;
the time's ill come fan ye'll be deid,
an' want naither meal nor breid.

The morn's the Timmer Market,
we'll a' be dressed in blue.
A reid ribbon in yer hair,
an' a sweetie in yer mou'.

Cabbies counted their tips by the Market Cross. Young assistants were told that it could not be a half and half split, for, 'The boss had the horsie to feed.'

Boxer Jock

Baith side o' a lane hung wi' claes,
maist o' them had seen better days;
been worn by the best in the lan'
but now for sale as second-han'.
On gey brae folk they might hae been seen
now in the Rag Fair o' Aberdeen.

Mrs Vinton and her staff outside the cafe at Rolland's Lodging. Built in 1535, it was the earliest known purpose-built tenement property in the city.

Rolland's Lodging, 38 Castle Street (on south side) was demolished in 1935. It had a vaulted basement and open fireplaces. Pitfodels Lodging, dated 1530, with three floors and turrets also stood in Castle Street as did the Earl

Marischal's Hall. This building however was two storeys high surrounding a courtyard; it made way for a new street to the harbour named in honour of his lordship. This involved the construction of a flyover in 1768.

PROCLAMATION OF KING GEORGE V. ABERDEEN. 10th MAY 1910. F.W.H.

12

CASTLEHILL

The original castle was destroyed by the Bruce party in 1308; what remains is in fact a Cromwellian bastion. A prominent feature on old engravings was the beacon at St. Ninian's Chapel on Castlehill. This building passed through a number of vicissitudes as a mortuary, a quakers' prison in the 1660s, when it was recorded that prisoners couldn't see their own food without the help of a candle, besides being blown up by the Jacobites. Professor Copland built an observatory there in 1781, near St. Ninian's Chapel. Both edifices were cleared away 1794–95 for the construction of the Barracks and powder magazine. The foundation stone was laid by the Duke of Gordon amid firing of field pieces, and vessels in the harbour were bedecked with flags. Six hundred men could be accommodated.

The differing styles of military uniform at Castlehill Barracks forecourt. The premises were later converted to flats for civilians before making way for high-rise housing. In 1881 a new building between the old building and the back of the Castle Street houses was opened for the accommodation of married soldiers.

The proclamation of King George V at the Mercat cross 10th May, 1910. On the Sovereign's birthday it was customary to light a bonfire, and men would haul a boat up Marischal Street to add to the conflagration at the Plainstanes. This two-step dais dates from 1752; the cross itself is late seventeenth century.

Robert Wilson sang in the Tivoli about the girl who wanted to be a Gordon's wife:

One day as I was walkin' in bonnie Aberdeen
I saw The Gordons marching in tartans gay and green;
beside me stood a lassie nae higher than my knee,
and as the lads ga'ed swinging by, that lassie said tae me:

Here's tae The Gordons, the lads who're staunch and true!
If I'd been a laddie, I'd been a Gordon too;
but seein' that I'm a lassie, I must be a lassie's life,
but one thing I'm determined on, is being a Gordon's wife.

COWGATE
From Justice Street to Park Street

Anciently, this was the tail end of an old drove road to the harbour and the grazing in the lands of Sandilands. It is last mentioned in the directories for the year 1892. By that time the quarter had become renowned for its 'unutterable squalor'. The access from Castlehill was improved in 1833. It had a row of small cottar-type houses with their backs to Commerce Street. It was a very narrow street wide enough for only one vehicle. 'The tenants had great difficulty in wet weather', mentions Marcus Milne, as the street level was higher than the pavement and the doors of the houses.

13

Gallowgate, looking towards Mounthooly, *c.* 1930.

GALLOWGATE
From Broad Street to Causewayend

'Ye must let folk ken that the Gallowgate wasn't a boring place at a'. I mind the clatter o' handcairts an' babble o' tongues heard in the sidestreets hitting the Gallowgate. Innes Street, and Young Street, ken. A' sorts o' interesting folk bade in Berry Street.'

The Gallowgate had everything going for east end folk; the Co-op Arcade, as well as a large variety of 'sma' shoppies', open late on Saturday nights. Advertisements on the Corporation buses assured shoppers that 'all roads lead to Browns' (where penny packets of tea were sold to the needy). Nardie's fish shop and Bendelow's pies with their 'fine het gravy' were local delicacies, whilst Greiggie's sweet shop was a 'shoppie o' hert whaur sweet rations were issued lang afore their time'. They sold 'smush' from the boilers—the 'chippit sweeties' left over after the 'hame made eens' had been put into the gleaming jars. Greiggie's cultivated a sweet tooth, because what they sold the 'loons and quines' was 'awfu' gweed'. Customers were also sure to admire the collection of toby jugs that dated back to the time of 'The Coughdrop Kings', sitting on the well stocked shelves.

There were plenty of brokers' shops, where anything from a 'demob suit' to tweed 'plus fours' could be purchased.

Pawn shops were a sign of the more solemn side of life here, and an inscription under a clock of one emporium read 'no tick here'. 'The Coopie divvie' was pawned for a half loaf, but somehow folk remained cheerful:

There was always a good film on at 'The Globie' for them to see, and jam jars were accepted for the price of a ticket. Bags of mixed broken biscuits were available as cheap refreshment. Outside, the ragman shouted 'tak' the stockings aff yer grannie's legs, the blankets aff yer mother's bed—toys for woollen rags'.

Mar's Castle (*c.* 1494) demolished for
street widening in 1897. There were
two archways at ground floor level
which led to an inner hall. At one time
there was a summer house and garden
at the back of 'The Castle'.

Pizzie Grant was 'a bonnie looking chiel'
and has a special niche in North East folklore.
As his portrait shows, he couldn't have been
'the height of a bobbie's crossbar'— even so,
he could carry weights of up to twenty stone.

First thing you bought at the Timmer Market was a 'pluffer' or peashooter and pelted passers bye with 'rodins' or rowantree berries when in season.

IN AUGUST FAIR I MAY BE SEEN,   WHERE YOUNG AND OLD ON PLEASURE BENT
IN THE CASTLEGATE O' ABERDEEN,   ENJOY THEMSELVES TAE THEIR HEART'S CONTENT.
MY NAME'S THE TIMMER MARKET.

The Porthill was the most northerly and highest of the three hills on which the 'Braif Toun' was built; and consequently the most exposed to the wind, which played freely round this echoing rookery.

Bairns would chant:

Rainie rainie rattle steens,
dinna rain on me.
Rain on Johnnie Groat's house,
far across the sea.

THE JUSTICE GATE

From Castlegate to Commerce Street and The Heading Hill

The Justice Port was built in 1440 at the east end of The Castlegate. Upon it were spiked the dismembered limbs of criminals. Nearby stood the Record Office, where the historic charters of the city were stored. The picturesque cottages with outside stairs have now been past history for a century, although they survived the demolition of the Port in 1787. The improvements of 1883 eradicated Sinclair's Close, Mauchlin Tower Court and Bothwell Court. 'I was struck with the horrid low appearance of the people in Justice Street where we lived,' wrote William Thom, the poet in 1826: 'The noise and brawling at night' caused him to travel to Dundee with his wife and family in search of work. This good-hearted man made a plea for 'the mitherless bairn':

Oh! speak him nae harshly he trembles the while
He bends to your bidding, and blesses your smile!
In their dark hour o' anguish, the heartless shall learn
that God deals the blow for the mitherless Bairn.

In Memoriam 'Jeems' (Pizzie) Grant

Ye min' hoo he cursed ye for ill-tricket geets,
an, chased ye thro' alleys, through bleachgreens and streets.
He ran like a deer, tho' his legs were but sma';

Fin ye shouted 'Pizzie' . . . but Pizzie's awa'.

I min' on the mannie since I wis a bairn,
I dinnae think that my stane wid be last on the cairn.

Let's rear a monument polished fu' braw
in mem'ry of 'Pizzie', 'cause Pizzie's awa!

(James Ogg)

Upper Kirkgate from Reid & Pearson's corner, Schoolhill. St. Nicholas Centre and St. Nicholas House now dominate the skyline.

NETHERKIRKGATE

From Broadgate to St. Nicholas Street

An early thirteenth century thoroughfare known then as 'the Road of the Ashtree'. Monks, and their retinue from Arbroath Abbey would be provided with 'shelter, fire, candlelight, bed and clothing'. Although the Hospital of St. Thomas that received the poor and infirm was swept away with it's gardens in 1770, you could 'ask for onything ye wintet' at Raggie Morrison's Bargain Store, that rose from the site. At Aberdeen's own 'Hudson Bay Trading Post', there were bundles of skins, frilly nightgowns, enamel basins, bolts of material and carpets there on 'the fleer', above which rose a spiral staircase in the middle of the shop; at the foot of which stood the haberdashery counter. Alert young ladies jumped to attention as customers approached, for they were paid on commission for every sale that they made from threads, ribbons, tapes, elastic, buttons, and cushion covers to be embroidered. North east needlewomen still retain some of the supplies that they invested in, even though 'Raggie's is awa''.

At the top of The Netherkirkgate stood the 'Round Table', a detached and rounded block of buildings in a crowded quarter. Half-way down the street stood the Netherkirkgate Port. Outside the port there was a spring well with an adjoining 'wellhouse', or 'wallhoose'; the most likely origin of the more modern Wallace Nook. Lord Byron, twenty-one years after leaving Aberdeen met a schoolfellow in Venice, and freely spoke of the haunts of his childhood, particularly mentioning Wallace Nook. In 1964, it was rebuilt stone by stone at Tillydrone.

Wallace Tower and the dislocated arm of The Netherkirkgate.

WALLACE

We'll miss the auld hoose wi' its toweries
   an' turrets,
The painter's abode near the fit o'
   Schoolhill;
We'll miss the wee windows an' quaint-
   lookin' garrets,
an' wish oor aul' frien' had been spared to
   us still

James Ogg refers to George Jamesone, the famous portrait painter. Born 1587, at School-hill, and sometimes known as 'the Van Dyke of Scotland'. The house stood opposite the grave-diggers' cottage and St. Nicholas Kirk.

19

UPPER KIRKGATE

**From the Broadgate to
St. Nicholas Street, but formerly
extending as far as Back Wynd**

The street runs west, just where the Gallowgate and Broadgate meet. It led through one of the ports to the upper gate of St. Nicholas Church and Blackfriars; hence the name. The ancient gate stood a little below Drum's Lane, and was carefully locked every night. One hundred and ninety years ago it was swept away. Although no engravings of it are known to exist, contemporary accounts state that it had a 'gallery' built over it, having apartments that connected with the houses on the north side. It was fashionable for merchants 'to bide at the top of The Broadgate,' but Provost Robertson's Lodging and Jamesone's House perished despite pleas of the preservationists.

Giuseppe Bordone, celebrated seller of hot chestnuts and icecream.

See him coming doon the street,
gymanastics on his feet;
the only man in Aiberdeen,
the only man to mak' icecream.

'YE BANKS AND BRAES'

This section would not have come about had it not been inspired by the lyrics that Robert Burns wrote, which appear frequently in the first line indexes of Scottish music anthologies; Indeed, his statue stands perched on the brink of 'Corby Heugh', where shetland ponies, (shelties), were at one time tethered on the unfenced woodland slope on 'the South Bank' of the Denburn, whilst their owners were away to the Castlegate Market.

John Ewen feued part of the lands of Ferryhill; he was a devotee of 'The Picturesque', a term in vogue at that time with landscape architects employed by wealthy landowners. Traces of his 'artistic designs, tasteful summer houses, winding walks embellished with statues and obelisks' may have given rise to the street names in the locality. The sense of wildness he wished to retain from the Pol Muir, with a plantation of fir woods and cowslip-covered banks belongs to the Scotland of Culloden, not the Duthie Park.

He established a silversmith's business in Castle Street, having travelled round the country from Montrose plying his trade. He gained respectability by undertaking a part time job from the Police Commissioners controlling the traders at the Castlegate Market. The ballad broadsheets were on sale for the benefit of those who wanted to learn the traditional songs, many of which had the title 'The banks of . . . ' then the name of the river concerned.

The street names associated with the Banks and Braes serve as a living reminder of the fields beneath the bland-looking buildings that now cover the contours of Aberdeen's underground burns, and the former floodplan of the River Dee.

The Corbie Well, named after the rookery which is still in existence on the wooded slopes of Union Terrace. Before the second Rosemount Viaduct was constructed, access to this spot was via Denburn Terrace off Skene Terrace.

AT THE CORBIE WELL,
UNION TERRACE GARDENS, ABERDEEN.
A DRAMA IN THREE ACTS.

Photo by Walker &

CATTLEBANK
From South College Street

This was the name given to the livestock loading bay adjacent to the Ferryhill railway junction.

CHERRYBANK AND GOOSEBERRYBANK

Property in Bon Accord Terrace. The latter is mentioned in a directory for 1853.

HOLLYBANK
From Hardgate to Holburn Street

This is a classic street of Aberdeen tenements. There is not a sprig of holly in sight.

ROSEBANK
At 133 Hardgate

This name belongs to an eighteenth century house now absorbed into the street line of Rosebank Place. It was formerly owned by the Dyce family before it was converted into a tenement; artists and literary men were frequent visitors. It was never as famous as 'Seaton Cottage', where artists such as Josef Israels were entertained. John Smith, the City Architect favoured Ferryhill as a place to stay, and resided at Rosebank until his death in 1852.

SPRINGBANK

As its name implies, it is a watershed between Crown Street and the Hardgate. Terrace housing complies with the contours of the land. Springbank Nursery was the beginning of the market gardens which stretched towards the Brig o' Dee from Bon Accord Street.

STRAWBERRYBANK

An early nineteenth century terrace at the top of the Hardgate

This attractive byeway with its attractive fan-light doors made way for garage extensions. At number seven, up the stairs was the Rosetti School of Music.

WILLOWBANK

This is the name given to the Regency house, Willowbank. It enjoyed an attractive prospect looking over the city. The Ferryhill Burn which powered the mill that formerly stood in the hollow of Albury Road had its pollution problems in 1878. The stench was described as 'a poison cloud'; the following verse is probably not an exaggeration.

Black and blae, yellow and long,
green and gruesome—and smelling strong.

I jogged awa' my aul' jog trot
tho' whiles beneath a thread-bare coat.
The chiel that disna' rise ava'
may rest content he'll never fa!

BROWNIE'S BRAE
From College Street to the Denburn

This street name has added charm due to the customary suffix of '-ie'; so beloved of Aberdonian diction. Even the grave loses its terror when referred to as 'a deid holie.' During the years 1831–3 there were constant complaints about the state of Brownie's Brae to the Police Commissioners. It is an old Scottish proverb that runs, 'When they're speaking about you they're not speaking about anybody else'. Now, the offending name has been expunged from the Street Directory. It sounded so innocent too. . . .

John Milne o' Livet's Glen.

CARNEGIE'S BRAE
From Netherkirkgate to East Green

The curbstones were originally laid in 1813. This brae was considered too steep for heavy laden carts, but somehow, the scaffie's cairt managed the ascent in a crab-like manner. 'The crap o' the causey' was put out to contract, but loons were on the lookout with their pail and shovel in the shadows of 'the Dark Briggie'. Carnegie was a dyer to trade, but there are more illustrious associations than these, for John 'Spanish' Phillip the Aberdeen-born artist was first apprenticed to a house painter in a cellar shop under the Wallace Tower. He is buried in Kensal Green cemetery, North London, where George Borrow who immortalised the Spanish gypsies also lies at rest. The Romany author visited Aberdeen on a six-hundred-mile walking tour in 1858, and entered upon 'some odd and entertaining conversation'. The date he noted down his observations was 5th November.

DOOCOT BRAE
From the Denburn Bleach Green to the 'Doocot'
A wee bit land . . .
a guid-gangin' plea;
a bundle o' debt
an' a doo-cot.

(respectability)

The Northern Assurance building occupies the site of the Doocot, but the present building is better known as the 'Monkey House'.

Corn grew in the fields where Aberdeen's New Town was built, and the pigeons filled their crops at the expense of tenant farmers only to replenish the larder of the Laird of Crimonmogate, when the *feu de joi* for the King's birthday was fired.

This vanished byeway gained notoriety as Sir John Cope's camping ground, but it was used by the Deeside and Donside Bonnet lairds whose shelts were tethered in the Denburn Wood known as 'Corbie Haugh'. Then, as now, the rooks are 'nae bonnie singers', and the merchandise was swiftly removed to the Castlegate Market where they had a deal with the wrights and joiners for their planks and spars. They also had regular customers for their hazel wands that made creels, birchback for tanning nets, ladders, caups, ladles, spigots and faucets. Pine root firelighters known as 'rosity reets' kept 'mony a lum fanning'.

FLOURMILL BRAE
From St. Nicholas Street to Barnett's Close

A well-kent money lender by the name of Lazurus Myres stayed here. His coats always had large pockets in which he carried jewellery, watches and silk goods. He sold elastic by the yard, taking care whilst measuring it to pull as hard as possible. He retired to Hamburg with his 'siller', hard-earned in Aberdeen. Raggie Morrison's in nearby Netherkirkgate in turn left their premises for Lord Seif to redevelop. Flourmill Brae has likewise vanished under the St. Nicholas Centre, and old Lazurus would not recognise his former haunts. There was a blacksmith and horse shoer at work in this street, and sparks were always flying.

Flourmill Brae, with demolition in progress at the back of Provost Skene's House and Flourmill Lane. The burn or 'aqueduct' which ran down from the Upper Mill is referred to in a deed of mortification by John Clat, in 1459. He founded St. Thomas' Hospital in The Netherkirkgate.

INCURABLE BRAE
From Upper Denburn to Baker Street

This was a steep, narrow lane that led from St. John's Croft nurseries to the Gilcomston Brae. 'Gilpie', as Gilcomstoun was affectionately referred to, was merged with the city upon the building of Rosemount and the South Mount Street viaducts. One of it's old landmarks, the Denburn Parish Church with it's rose window still stands out, but Belleville cottage, later converted and enlarged in 1866 and 1877 as a hospital for 'incurables' was demolished a century ago and the establishment removed to Morningfield.

JACK'S BRAE
From Upper Denburn to Leadside Road

Echoed with the clatter of looms; for weavers produced cottons, linens, haircloth and tapes in their sheds. This was a cottage industry. Gilcomston Mill and the weaving shed in Blair's Lane, Leadside Road were the last of the Jack's Brae properties to be cleared in 1984.

The street was named after John Jack in 1758.

Weavers wore tall hats in which they could carry the pirns to the loom. On Friday they took 'the wob' to the merchant.

I wadna' marry a weaver ava, ava. It's pirns to fill at four o'clock in the morn. . . .

Looking up Jack's Brae.

The Incurable Brae looking towards Rosemount. The viewpoint is the high garden ground at the corner of Summer Street and Skene Street. The houses of Stevenson Street, erected in 1880 by W. S. Stevenson, tea merchant, are seen on the left, and Ledingham's corner on Rosemount is another landmark.

THE LANG BRAE

From Skene Street, in line with Summer Street, to the Upper Denburn. Now an anonymous flight of stairs

Miss Cushnie's School was at the foot of the Brae; when the burn was in spate, she was unable to receive her scholars. It is recorded that when 'she bocht in grey peas and biled them' there were no absentees.

The Spring Well of St. John of Jerusalem was removed from the environs of Upper Denburn and Lang Brae to a landscaped garden outside the headquarters of the order, in Albyn Place.

MONKEY BRAE

From Prospect Terrace to Wellington Suspension Bridge

Officially known as Wellington Brae, it led down to the Craiglug ferry. Its main users were foundry workers who lived in cottages amidst the policies of Old Ferry hill House. Within living memory there was a wee shoppie at the arch under the railway. The proprietor and his pet monkey are now one of the legends of Aberdeen.

'It's half twal'.' The night patrol shouted out the quarter hours and a weather report.

THE MUTTON BRAE

From Woolmanhill to Denburn

There are two explanations given as to why the brae got its name. The first being that the woolmarket was held nearby—the second being that this was the route by which the postillions took the carriages to call for the Belmont Street society women, who got themselves a reputation as being 'mutton dressed up as lamb'. Clachan folk encouraged their lassies to be humble and enjoy the simple things in life like 'mony a guid air' from the resident fiddler who would serenade them under the Provost's Plane Tree in the Corbie Well Heugh.

The spire of the Triple Kirks, (Archibald Simpson 1844), was built of granite, but clad with second-hand bricks, made locally at Clayhills. The inspiration for the design came from the twin-spired cathedral at Marburg in Germany. Taking the measurements from basement level in Denburn Road, this is said to be the second highest spire in Great Britain.

When the railway was built over the course of the Denburn, a test to see if vibration would cause any danger to the Triple Kirks' foundations necessitated tumblers of water to be placed in doorways. 'Whistling was not allowed as the train went into the tunnel'. When the spire required inspection, James Wright, the original steeplejack, who had scaled Britain's highest spire (that of Salisbury Cathedral) showed how swiftly he could proceed, once the two strings of his kite were on opposite sides of the Steeple, as he spliced on heavier lines to carry him upwards within the hour.

Mrs Ledingham, who kept a bar on the right-hand side of the brae coming from the Denburn this was the first howff inside the city, coming from the direction of Gilcomston. Mary Slessor, the famous missionary who was born in Mutton Brae, saw washing cut down on 'fast days'.

SHORE BRAE
From the Quay to Shiprow

This was a short street, with the last of its projecting houses demolished in 1795. It was the chief access to the old harbour before the Georgian and Victorian improvements, which removed a deep pool in the vicinity which was known as the Pottie. Criminals were drowned there by means of a wooden crane.

It may be this folklore tradition that named the Shiprow lavatories the Forty Pots.

There was puir bar'fit Jeams, wha the loons
did torment,
Till ane aifter th' ither to the 'head place' he
sent,
But each as they passed him they gave him a
dig—
They were devilish loons on the auld Bow
Brig.
When manhood approached them, they a'
slipped awa—
Some gaed to the sea, some the plough for
to ca';
Ithers went to Australia, their fortunes to
dig,
And forsook a' their pranks at the auld Bow
Brig.
The toon cooncillors came, when the loons
were frae hame,
Tore doon the auld brig (oh! mair to their
shame);
Had the loons been there, faith, "the man
wi' the wig"
Durstnae touched but ae stane o' the auld
Bow Brig.
But it's jist whit they dae wi' the puir
workin' man—
Och, they tear him to pieces as soon as they
can;
But stap them th'gither, wi' their bellies sae
big,
They could raise nae sic biggin' as the auld
Bow Brig.

Monkey Brae, Aberdeen (Winter).

The Windmill, which gave the street it's
name dated from 1680. It had the
commanding site in Crown Terrace that the
Baptist church now occupies, and became
known as Johnny Cope's Watchtower to
commemorate the occasion when two
thousand soldiers entered Aberdeen from the
north in September 1748. When Drumgarth, a
Deeside Villa at Pitfodels was being
landscaped, the owner set up the tower as a
summerhouse, minus its sails.

In 1850, there was a plan to have a grand
entrance archway to the railway in Romanesque style by the local architect James
Henderson, on the slope where the Palace
Hotel was subsequently built. With the recent
demolition of the last of the old Windmill
Brae houses adjacent to the Royal Hotel, and
the concrete advent of the Trinity Centre, a
few words concerning the life of the
community at the 'fit o'' the Windmill Brae
wouldn't come amiss, mainly because changes
in Victorian Aberdeen were carefully
chronicled by minor poets and unofficial
historians. They were uncannily prophetic, as
bridges with as beautiful lines as the Old Bow
Brig have only survived by and large inside
country estates.

Shoudie poudie
pair of new sheen;
up The Gallowgate
and doon The Green.

WINDMILL BRAE

From College Street to Crown Street

Official Receptions and farewells to important visitors to the town from the south
were made here, because at that time Union
Street and Holburn Street did not exist. This
thoroughfare which linked up with Hardgate,
continued on over the Denburn, by way of the
old Bow Brig, into the Green.

This single-arched bridge was designed by
the first known Aberdeen 'architect', John
Jeans, and erected in 1747. It survived for just
over a century, and made way for the Denburn Valley Railway footbridge which had a
longer lifespan, having been rationalised as
part of The Trinity Centre (1983); relics from
the Old Bow Brig were taken to Union Terrace
Gardens.

THE GREEN

Anciently from Windmill Brae to Putachieside. Now from East Green to Denburn Road and the Trinity Centre

G. M. Fraser thought fit to write a mono-
graph on the subject. Archaeologically the
area has yielded some important finds, but it
is the institution of the Green, not architecture
that endears the place to the true Aberdonian.

THE GREEN, ABERDEEN.

The Cove fisherwomen at the head of the Green. On the left is Hadden's Mill. The footbridge over the railway is prominent. The Denburn had to be culverted following the removal of the Old Bow Brig. There is now a Darker Briggie at the entrance to Denburn Road, than at the other end of the Green at Carnegie's Brae. Before the access to the railway bridge was changed, the tidal water of the Denburn could be seen six feet below the garage which made way for Littlewoods' extension.

Two orders of Friars had monasteries in the Green, the Trinitarians and the Carmelites. The Trinitarians, or Red Friars, was on the angle between Market Street and Guild Street, while the Carmelites, or White Friars resided in the south west angle of the Green, having the Denburn on the west and south.

The Green Market has always been well stocked from local allotments. 'Fresh butter, country cheese and eggs hot from the nest' are street cries of the olde-time traders.

The overhead sign outside Adam's shop was an outsize teapot capable of pouring mony a fly cup.

THE WYNDS

AEDIE'S WYND

From Shiprow to the Netherkirkgate

This street formed the connecting link between the lower ends of the Shiprow and the Netherkirkgate. It is one of the lost streets of Aberdeen, and enjoyed a western exposure on the side of St. Katherine's Hill. In winter it became ideal for 'makin' a slidie'.

Andrew Aedie's Lodging built by Andrew Jamesone, master mason, was the last of the Green's ancient houses, and stood beside Back Wynd Stairs. It was demolished in 1914, and its site has remained vacant ever since. It had the dubious reputation of being the Kidnapper's House where the operation to sell children into slavery was master-minded. Peter Williamson, born in Hirnlay near Aboyne, was eleven years old when he was kidnapped. After many incredible adventures encompassing escape from slavery and torture by Huron Indians, he eventually returned to Aberdeen and exposed the evil practice. The last proprietor of the shoppie on the ground floor was John Buchan, but Back Wynd Stairs have no connection with the author of *The Thirty-nine Steps*.

'The Mannie', now in The Castlegate, was relegated to the Green for many years. William Lindsay, designer of the Fountainhead (1708), intended water to play and issue from the leaden statue, and four antique faces. There are two other statues in the world that are just as ingenious: Eros in Piccadilly Circus, London, and the Manikin Pis in Brussels.

BACK WYND

From Union Street to Schoolhill

Laid out by the magistrates in 1594, this street gave access to the west side of the kirk by way of the Green. In the days that it was known as Westerkirkgate, the graveyard was partially enclosed with houses. The major alteration was the construction of Union Street, which truncated vehicular access from the Green. The cassies from the old street can still be seen near Back Wynd Stairs. Aberdeen appointed

it's first 'cassay' or 'calsay' maker in June 1539. This is the second flight of stairs to have surmounted the storage vaults under Union Street.

A feature of the street has long been the back of the baroque monuments, and festoons of blossom complementing the stone swags. A cautionary tale has been recorded concerning a youth who was wrongfully accused of stealing fruit from these trees. For this, he was locked in 'the Pity Vault', and rats gnawed him to death.

'Yella haddies, tasty kippers, tippence a pair; five for fourpence.' Finnan haddies were originally made famous as a delicacy by the villagers of Findon. These country fisher lassies had their own stance mid way down the Green. In the background can be seen the New Market. Some walked home with a creel full of provisions that took two men to strap it onto their backs.

Beggars in the town attended better-class funerals. The beadle came out with a plate of halfpennies and distributed one to each of them. Willie Milne had to be watched as he tried to change his position in the queue as often as he could.

The funeral of Lady Anderson on 17th December 1886 seemed to signify the end of an era, when Sir Alexander, aged eighty-five, in feeble health, followed his wife's coffin to the graveside in a sedan chair, carried by two shore porters. A well wisher asked the old advocate if he was feeling better and was told: 'I'll be no better laddie till I get to the kingdom of Heaven', and turned away. He got there on 11th April 1887.

Back Wynd Stairs were flanked with old houses left and right. Their back yards met the graveyard wall of St. Nicholas before Union Street was constructed.

Nae a single grave-steen in St. Nicholas Kirkyard,
Hap it gentle or simple, Provost, Preacher or Bard,
But he'll tell you the story o' wha lies beneath,
Whar he first saw the licht; whar he drew his last breath:
What he did; what he left; was there Love in his heart;
Did he help the down-trodden and play a man's part:
If he did, then be sure his life record will glow
Like a glint of sweet sunshine, through Saunders Munro

(W. Carnie)

James Harvey was mason in charge of erecting the granite steeple of the kirk in 1875, and deserves as much credit as the then City Architect for his work. The Gothic immensity of the structure overshadows Drum's and Collison's Aisles, which have been through as many vicissitudes as the old East and West Kirks. The lead from the latter's roof was sold to the Netherlands in 1742, four years later it

The Pynours at the East Kirk of St. Nicholas

was utilised as a provender store by the Duke of Cumberland's army. By 1755 it had been rebuilt to designs by James Gibbs (more properly known as Gibb), who for his part was made 'Free Guild Brother Burgess'. He was compiler of *The Book of Architecture* (1728), and the church colonial architects. The rusticated windows are known as Gibbs' Windows, and it is appropriate that they yet exist today in his home town. London may have the famous Academy of St. Martin In The Fields which is known for its musical excellence. Aberdeen ensured the quality of the 'Toun's Music' by having a Song School attached to the Kirk. Thus the city can be seen to be a pioneer of music festivals. Carillon concerts are also a highlight. The Latin translation from the oldest bell reads:

Lo, I the bell do not proclaim the praise of
    that which is unholy;
I glorify the creator, I draw away the fear of
    thunder,
I mourn in solemn tones the departed,
I tell of the recurrent rites of faith,
I move the heart of the man who is joyful.
behold me, I am Lawrence!

    Sticks and steens
    will brak' my beens,
    but names winna harm me;
    but fan I'm deid
    an' in my grave
    ye'll mind fit ye caed me.

Lang Willie Milne.

GEO. LITTLEJOHN & CO., BACK WYND, ABERDEEN
ORDERS FOR BRECHAM COLLARS ESTEEMED

Littlejohn's shop in Back Wynd sold silver-topped whips to livery stables.

FOWLER'S WYND
From the Green to Fisher Row

This street at one time of day was the main road into the city from the south. It has vanished, along with the adjacent Fisher Row.

FUTTIE'S WYND
From Castle Terrace to Virginia Street

Once known as Hangman's Brae, a convenient short cut 'up the Toon' for 'trachled' fishwives. The story goes that whilst the Town Clerk was actively threatening redundancy to the hangman, the latter challenged him to a duel. Town Planning belatedly responded, by cutting first, Castle Terrace, and later a ring road through the kailyards adjoining 'the Hangman's but 'n' ben', thus eradicating his house, and 'executing' Hangman's Brae. In the vicinity was Angel's Brae, which ran from Castle Terrace to Commerce Street. There were no angels, but anatomy students dealt directly with the hangman, because he was the only official from whose hands a corpse could lawfully be procured.

Futtie's Myre Croft house was adapted to become Aberdeen's first Masonic Lodge building. Its 'thackit' roof was at the mercy of tempests besieging the Heading Hill. This did not detract members, however.

GARVOCK WYND
From Garvock Street to the Links

Formerly an ancient drove road that led from St. Fotin's Chapel to a watering place at the back of the Links. Now it is Lawrence Garvock, a provost, that is remembered, not St. Fotin.

CORRECTION WYND
From St. Nicholas Street to the Green

This is the only street now in use that cut into the Green, on the northern side prior to the formation of Union Street. The Public Soup Kitchen was situated in St. Mary's chapel (1800–35). We are told that the copper kettle weighed eight pounds; the salt and pepper used to season thirty-three weeks' broth cost £10 7s. with an additional £5 13s. 4d. for cooking it. Ingredients consisted of barley, beef, peas and vegetables. Three rolls cost a penny. Priest Gordon was frequently seen 'ladlin oot' soup. He was a fine man, an' weel liket.' I wonder if he got nearer their herts with "the meat that perisheth" rather than by "the words o' eternal life".'

Dr Ferguson the druggist, on the other hand, had a number of creatures suspended in glass jars that could be seen through the window of his shop at the head of the Green. He encouraged children to bring him their grubs, piebald snails and dragonflies. During the second half of the seventeenth century, magistrates sent to the House of Correction, here in 'The Correction House Wynd,' 'all vagabonds, strong and sturdie beggares, idle and maisterless persones; strong in bodie and habitt to work. Servants disobedient to maistris, children disobedient to parentis. Leud leivars, pyikers, common scaldies and uncorrigible harlottis not amending to the discipline of the kirk'. The kirkyard wall cut out much of the daylight. Advocates' offices in garrets looked out over the tombs.

NARROW WYND
From Union Street to Castle Street

This formed the southern approach to the Castlegate, and was finally cleared in 1867. Its forestairs were removed in 1796 when it was 'paved with square stones.' The south side was cleared in 1806, so that Union Street engineering works could proceed. The last of the houses were taken down for the Townhouse extensions in the 1860s. It's name had been given to a friendly society founded in 1660, so it hasn't finally gone beyond our ken. Those who attended their meeting rooms there included silk dyers, soap boilers, flax dressers, saddlers, skinners, coach makers, farmers and stay makers, who paid the annual subscription of two shillings, a crown upon their wedding, and a shilling for each child of their marriage.

RENNIE'S WYND
From the Green to Trinity Street

This was the Denburn 'cairters' route to the station yard. Hadden's Mill (1805) gave the place the air of an L. S. Lowrie painting. The proprietors of The Carmelite Friar's garden which lay adjacent, agreed to widen what was then called 'Baillie Strachan's Wynd' opposite to the friar's kiln and small barns. These barns were said to have been used for holding children against their will, with the intention of selling them off into slavery.

WINDY WYND
From Gallowgate to Spring Garden

This was a track that followed the northern bank of the dwindling Loch of Aberdeen.

Inside The House of Correction.

> It's twal'o' clock,
> the ghaist appears;
> we'll a' ging doon the stair—
> an' fan we see the bogie man
> we'll get an awfu' scare.

ST. KATHERINE'S WYND
From Union Street to Netherkirkgate

It formerly was the northern 'brae' of St. Katherine's Hill which was levelled by Georgian navvies, who at the same time cleared an island wedge of buildings known as the Round Table, when Union Street was constructed. The present streetline dates from 1810.

THE ROWS

DUBBIE ROW
From Putachieside to St. Nicholas Kirk

Dubbie Row, well named, can no longer be found. It was given up in 1806, and it's best public draw well removed two years later. It was a hazard for man and beast alike, despite improvements in 1795. As recently as 1865 the Loch stream provided power for a meal mill, but even it runs unseen now below ground to the Dark Briggie. It seems appropriate that the first Victorian braille handbook, *Light on Dark Paths* to be printed in the city, was compiled in the locality of Dubbie Row.

Exchequer Row, prior to modern development.

'The Long Bar', Castle Street.

EXCHEQUER ROW
From Castle Street to Shiprow

Exchequer Row or the 'Chacker Raw' as it was alternatively known, was originally the street where the Mint was situated. This was a narrow thoroughfare into which the sun seldom penetrated. The houses towered above the quays like the enormously high old Lands of Edinburgh.

JOHN JAMIESON, LANG BAR, CASTLE STREET

Gardens that ran in blossom to the quays became covered with 'the most squalid dens in Europe'. Backyards were sodden with garbage and windows stuffed with rags by the time the demolition men moved into Burnett's House, and found wine vaults under the seventeenth-century building and a mummified cat in the eaves to ward off evil spirits. Robert Burnett, a merchant who held high office was allowing seamen to use an underground passage from the shore to his secret store, and how long smuggling continued after his death is not known. This may be the reason why Mrs Affleck kept wildfowl in the 'Shallie Close' which led through to Virginia Street, so that they could act as a lookout for strangers. She also kept an eagle in a cage and monkeys chained to posts. The close itself was decorated by Robert Stronach, a wright, who used to collect shells off the beach and carry them home in the deep pockets of his blue greatcoat. He painted them various colours and decorated the walls of his tenement with grotesque patterns. Alexander Leslie owned the Mint Building.

FISHER ROW
From the Green and Maltmill Brig to Shiprow

This was the now vanished route to old Trinity Hall from the Green. It was a narrow thoroughfare which was widened in 1795. Skirting the old boatyards, it was inevitable that there would be tradesmen working in the vicinity, such as a sawyer, cooper, millwright and vintner. An artificial limb maker, baker and weaver are also listed in the archives. There is no mention of a candlestickmaker however. 'Tasties' were served by the kerb-side here: 'Caller dulse tae cha' a penny a bowlie'. This was long tender tangles of sea-weed that hissed as it cooked in a blackened iron pan, as 'wee beasties' were scorched with a hot poker and served with vinegar and chips.

GUESTROW
From Netherkirkgate to Upperkirkgate

The Guestrow was one of the earliest streets in Aberdeen (1439). Although it still survives in part as a narrow thoroughfare beside a municipal lock-up carpark, it was never part of a larger Broadgate, because a burn ran between them.

In academic circles for certain, the street became a bye-name for good printing. Students, who didn't study their set books, were to be found in the underground shooting gallery where they passed the time of day with hardened carriers who fortified themselves in passing time at Mother Robertson's New Inn with two-penny nips of 'Kill the Cairter' raw whisky. The game of 'Shooting for spoons' preceded the era of the Guestrow Carnivals which made use of the demolition sites occasioned by the clearance of old property. In October 1932, Mr Fraser heard about the demolition of the shooting gallery and came to see it's painted panels which resembled stage scenery, for the last time. He interviewed 'a pleasant-faced woman about thirty; she wore spectacles, and in answer to his questions said, "It's been an old house since ever I remember, the Shootin' Gallery wis afore my time."' He wrote down the pleasantries in his jotting book. How long had she lived there? 'A' my days,' she answered. 'You were born here?' 'Aye, wis I that,' she replied.

Courtesy to strangers didn't pass with the going of the provosts and dukes that used to occupy these old houses. The 'Gush', as it became known, never sent the needy away without meat. 'We'll give ye a crust but nae saxpence,' was their saying. There was also a 'dispensary lying-in vaccine institutions' near by in Barnett's Close for those patients whose houses were too wretched for them to receive proper attention.

The House of Refuge was opened at Cumberland House in spring 1836. Its objects were expressed by Mr Brown of St. Paul's Episcopal Chapel in the Gallowgate, who trusted that this would be 'a temporary shelter for the destitute'. Under the watchful eye of Elizabeth Pirie, inmates could cook their own food and have a good old-fashioned news. Upstairs, in apartments that had at one time of day been bonnie, the beds were lumpy.

Funerals in the Guestrow were an event

 Blin' Bob.

which nevertheless attracted a great amount of public notice in Aberdeen. When Duncan Campbell McKinlay, better known as 'Blin' Bob' died on 8 March 1889, thousands of spectators turned out. Mr Max Gregor of Marischal Street took a plaster cast of McKinlay's head which was found to be 23½ inches in circumference. Had he been possessed of eyesight and education there was no doubt that he would have been a man holding down a good job. The 'Ironmonger's mask' however was larger than the plaster cast previously mentioned. It serves as a reminder of a quarrel between two tradesmen. The likeness of Alexander Stephen is now firmly fixed to the tower of Provost Skene's House, nearest the archway under St. Nicholas House. The other sculpture by Russett has disappeared. It was said that 'the artist in gargoyles used under-done pork and porter suppliers to achieve his masterpieces'. Whatever they said about him, the scavengers of Aberdeen could keep out the cold with a 'bowlie o' soup and a maskin o' tea' thanks to Russett's munificence in his will.

Shiprow looking towards Exchequer Row and the Townhouse. Narrow lanes, running between the garden walls between Shiprow and Castle Street were given the name, Back Traps. The last of the old hawthorne trees that once covered St. Catherine's Hill survived in Abbey Place until *c.* 1912.

The Lemon Tree Hotel, Huxter Row. The houses fronting those in Huxter Row are the remnants of the Narrow Wynd which was part of a wedge of buildings cleared for the construction of Union Street. The gentlemen wearing stovepipe hats are town officials who are following up the eviction notices which were served on 26 January 1867.

39

HOSPITAL ROW
From St Andrew Street to Blackfriars Street

This was the name given to the western end of St. Andrew Street as defined by the high wall surrounding Robert Gordon's College (otherwise known as Hospital).

HUXTER ROW
From Broad Street to Castle Street

A short street off the Broadgate; its site now taken up entirely by the Townshouse. It was a business place with lock-up shops or booths; the exchange of the town. The booths in which the dealers used to display small articles for sale gave this historic place its name. The original Lemon Tree Hotel stood here, but with the labyrinth of courts it perished *c.* 1867. Aberdeen had a very-flourishing book-selling and publishing fraternity in the nineteenth century, and their social life was centred upon the hotel, where their suppers were served in homely surroundings. These were convivial occasions, but bad language was stamped out; however the last bawdy laugh belongs to the lady who appealed to the Lord Provost, Magistrates and councillors, concerning the eviction notice that she had received. Her requirements were simple, that she be allowed to take away 'the almost indispensable commode, my water closet, which would be of little value to the said gentlemen, and might be very useful to me'. 'The Said Gentlemen' spared no expense for that department at the new Townshouse, which was finished in 1872. The accommodation for the chosen few even excels the 'Royal Loo' at Union Terrace.

☛ The corner of the Broadgate and Huxter Row. The turret design may be familiar; it has been adapted for the Town House clock tower.

ROTTEN ROW
From Union Street to Guestrow

'The Route de Roi', the approach to The Townshouse used by visiting royalty. A small lane adjoining the Guestrow; its line enclosed in a department store extension. Anciently its name was Rattin Row because the houses were not all stone—but boarded. By 1796 some of the houses were ruinous; the south end being built over. By 1805 there were remonstrations that the thoroughfare hadn't been given the precedence that Correction House Wynd had received, by being given an archway through to Shiprow. It remained unarched and given the more metropolitan-sounding name 'Union Lane' in 1824.

Along the front of the building yards in the Upper Dock was ranged a line known as Rotten Row (not to be confused with the one in Hyde Park London). It was worn out disused schooners and brigs. A broom at the masthead indicated that the ship could be made fit for sea duty. This sad sight increased in the 70's with the advent of steam.

SHIPROW
From Union Street to Trinity Corner

'The Provost stood at the door of his house, and he counted the ships on the tide.' Shipmasters and shore porters lived here in sight of the ships, and from Provost Ross' House (The Maritime Museum), a clear view of work on board can still be seen. In terms of how the Toun of New Aberdeen developed, this street could claim to be the oldest. Near the Shore Brae stood the Trinity or Quay Head Port, and was the most direct road to the harbour and shipping. Today Provost Ross' name is foremost, but Provost Robert Davidson should likewise be associated; he led his fellow citizens on the battlefield of Harlaw. This ballad enjoyed a revival when it was heard in all its glory sung by Jeannie Robertson.

An eviction in Shiprow c. 1876. A policeman is present, demolition work on the building is proceeding regardless.

Besides keeping a wineshop, Robert Davidson was a leading merchant and had another place of business in Shiprow. John Ross, the Provost after which the early seventeenth-century house is named, actually took up residence in 1782. Attempts were made to make the vicinity more sophisticated. In 1796, two wooden fronted houses were taken down for street widening, and 'forestairs' demolished. As late as 1822 there was a wooden tenement. It was life in a tenement here that no doubt influenced the song-writing of Mary Brooksbank who was born here in December 1897. Her father was one of the founder members of The Aberdeen Docker's Union, and was himself a dock labourer. Her mother worked as a domestic servant when she wasn't earning extra coppers as a fish worker. In Mary's modest autobiography, she allows the soft light from a pair of cherished candlesticks that cast strange shadows on the roof and corners of that well-scrubbed tenement kitchen, to linger on for posterity.

Shiprow looking towards Market Street, *c*.1876. The houses on the right, facing down Shore Brae were taken down to build the Trinity Congregational Church (1878). Fragments of sixteenth-century masonry survive nearby. The original thirteenth-century hilltop chapel of St. Catherine of Sienna had its entrance gate somewhere in this vicinity.

Provost Ross's House was saved after years of neglect in December 1952. It dates from 1593, the work of Andrew Jamesone. In the foreground is the Shiprow Stairs leading to the Shiprow Union United Free church, built in 1822. It later became known as Shiprow Tavern, a Temperance establishment with the motto, Faith, Hope and Charity. Its sign was a full-rigged ship.

THE COURTS AND CLOSES

Only 21 Remain

Abbey Place 46 Shiprow
Albion Court 17 Castle Street
Allardyce's Court 54 Castle Street
Anderson's Court 22 Upperkirkgate
Anderson's Court 46 Loch Street
Annand's Court 30 James Street
Bank of Scotland Court 35 Castle Street
Barnett's Close Guestrow to Flourmill Brae
  (carried right through, 1778)
Beattie's Court 99 & 102 Gallowgate
Bede House
Blackbull Close 4 Huxter Row
Booth's Court 66 Upperkirkgate
Bourtie's Court 29 Upperkirkgate
Boy's Hospital Court 19 Upperkirkgate
Brebner's Court 84 Shiprow
Brebner's Court Castle Street (later spelt
  'Bremner')
Bruce's Court 22 Loch Street
Burn Court 44 Upperkirkgate
Burnett's Close 5 Exchequer Row
Burr's Court 152 Gallowgate
Bursar's Court 61 Castle Street
Cameron's Court 30 North Street
Candle Court 51 Loch Street
Candlemaker's Court 46 Gallowgate
Chapel Court 1 Justice Street
Chapel Court 61 Gallowgate
Charles Court 40 Upperkirkgate
Cheyne's Court 69 Broad Street
Chronicle Court 32 Broad Street &
  10 Queen Street
Clark's Court 2 Upperkirkgate
Clune's Court 75 George Street
College Court 82 Broad Street
Collie's Court 28 Shiprow
Collie's Court 60 Gallowgate
Commercial Court 58 Castle Street
Concert Court 10/12 Broad Street
(Weekly concerts were given here by the
  Aberdeen Musical Society (1747)
Cooper's Court 26 Netherkirkgate
Courage's Court 2 Weighhouse Square
Coutt's Close Wallace Nook, Netherkirkgate
Craigmile Court 59/61 Commerce Street
Crombie's Court 37 Park Street
Crown Court 41½ Union Street

Crown Court 36 Upperkirkgate
Cruden's Court 22 Broad Street
(Named after Alexander Cruden, author of
  The Biblical Concordance)
Cruikshank's Court 46 Shiprow
Cruikshank's Court 8 Schoolhill
Cruikshank's Court 91 Broad Street
Daniel's Court 48 Castle Street
Davidson's Court 113 Gallowgate
Dingwall's Court 85 Gallowgate
Donald's Close 14 Schoolhill
Donald's Court 16 Loch Street
Downie's Court 65 Broad Street
Duncan's Court 45 Castle Street
Duncan's Court 120 Gallowgate
Duncan's Court 74 Gallowgate
Duthie's Court 45 Guestrow
Duthie's Court 14 Schoolhill
Duthie's Court 41 Virginia Street
Emslie's Court 81 George Street
Emslie's Court 26 Gallowgate
Ewen's Court 42 Gallowgate
Exchange Court 35–37 Union Street
Exchequer Court 9 Exchequer Row
Factory Court 59 George Street
Farquhar's Court 16 Upperkirkgate
Farquarson's Court 10 Schoolhill
Ferguson's Court 108½ Gallowgate
Forbes Court 78 The Green
Galen's Court 21 Guestrow
Garrow's Court 8 Trinity Street
Garden's Court 15 Castle Street
Geddes Court 17 Prince Regent Street
Gibb's Court 91 Shiprow
Gordon's Court 22 Gordon Street
Gordon's Court 4 Schoolhill
Gordon's Court 43 Virginia Street
Gordon's Court 75 Queen Street
Gordon's Court 88 Broad Street

Galens Court was demolished in 1935, but the archway here dating back to 1673, the pride and joy of Agnes Divie whose house it gave access to has been re-erected after its travels to Union Terrace Gardens in front of Provost Skene's House, not far away from its original site.

Grant's Court 38 West North Street
Grant's Court 49 Upperkirkgate
Greig's Court Windmill Brae
Harper's Court 76 West North Street
Harvey's Court 98 Gallowgate
Hay's Court Trinity Corner
Henderson's Court 91, 123 & 161 Gallowgate
Henderson's Court 46 Broad Street
Hutcheon's Court 4 Shiprow
Inglis Court 30 Gallowgate
Ironmonger's Court 14 Upperkirkgate
Jaffray's Court 51 North Street
Jamieson's Court 5 Upperkirkgate
Jamieson's Court 38 Shiprow
Jopp's Court 31 Gallowgate
(Named after Alex. Jopp, manager of
  Aberdeenshire Canal office)
Jopp's Court 40 Broad Street and 11 Queen
  Street
Kilgour's Court 46 Netherkirkgate
Knox's Court 7 Wales Street
Lamb's Court 5 Putachie-side
Lamond's Court 49 Upperkirkgate
Ligertwood's Court 99 George Street
Lobban's Court 29 Castle Street
Logan's Court 152 Gallowgate
Luxemburg Close Castle Street to West
  North Street & Long Acre
Machray's Court 81 George Street.
Machray's Court 13 Bon Accord Street
Matheson's Court 15 Castle Street
Mathieson's Court 9 Constitution Street
Mearn's Court 53 Shiprow
Melville's Court 106 Gallowgate
Messon's Court 31 Justice Street
Meter's Court 11 Chapel Lane
Milne's Court 27 Gallowgate
Milne (Provost) Court, 65 Gallowgate
Milner's Court 25 Guestrow
Milner's Court 38 Castle Street
Mitchell's Court 41 Guestrow
M'Combie's Court 50½ Union Street to 51
  Netherkirkgate (opened 1812)
M'Cook's Court 116 Gallowgate
M'Gregor's Court 99 Gallowgate
M'Kay's Court 80 Gallowgate (Closed 1918)
  (Otherwise known as 'The Can'le Closie)

'Pit yer feet roun' The Kypie'. Playing
bools outside Provost Skene's House.
There were different types of bools:
'canons' (double shots), 'mexies',
'changies', 'tattie mashers', 'ironers'
and 'claysers'; the latter being used in
iron kettles to avoid lining.

The motto over the door reads,
'Thanks be to God'. Sir George Skene,
who chose his words carefully, died in
1707. They gained added emphasis
when the Culloden campaign
occupation of his house was over in
1746.

M'Kay's Court 18 Trinity Street
M'Kenzie's Court 42 George Street
M'Lean's Court 50 Gallowgate
Moir's Court 103 Gallowgate
Morrison's Court 2 Fisher Row
National Bank Court 42 Castle Street
Neptune Terrace 47 York Street
Nicol's Court 106 John Street
Niven's Court 29 Guestrow
Ogston's Court 84 Broad Street
Oliver's Court 12 Upperkirkgate
Painter's Court 22 Upperkirkgate
Patagonian Court Belmont Street to
  Denburn Road
Peacock's Close 24 Castle Street. (Named
  after a dancing master)
Pensioner's Court 18 Justice Street
Petrie's Court, 50 The Green
Philipp's Court 147 Gallowgate
Pirie's Court 50 Castle Street
Pirie's Court 1 Upperkirkgate
Plasterer's Court 70 Gallowgate
Poor's Hospital Court 56 Gallowgate
Porter's Court 12 Weigh House Square
Porthill Close 98 Gallowgate
Quaker's Court 55 Guestrow
Ramage's Court 83 Broad Street to
  Guestrow
Ramsay's Court 57 Guestrow
Red Lion Court 77 Broad Street to
  Guestrow
Reid's Court 34 Gallowgate
Reid's Court 49 Gallowgate
Reid's Court 7 Shiprow
Rettie's Court 26 Broad Street
Rhind's Court 64 Gallowgate
Riddel's Court 40 Windmill Brae
Robertson's Court 46 Netherkirkgate
Roper's Court 107 Gallowgate & 47 Loch
  Street
Rose's Court 18 Commerce Street
Ross' Court 22 Schoolhill
Ross' Court 11 Trinity Corner
Ross' Court 6 Upperkirkgate

Salter's Court 50 Lochside
Scott's Court 25 Regent Quay
Seaton's Court 91 Broad Street
Sharp's Court 78 Loch Street
Shaw's Court 90 Gallowgate
Shewan's Court 119 Gallowgate
Shipmaster's Court 97 Shiprow
Shuttle Court 16 East North Street
Simpson's Court 139 Gallowgate
Sinclair's Close 20 Justice Street
Smith's Court 16 Netherkirkgate
Smith's Court 113 Gallowgate
Smith's Court 21 Castle Street
Stewart Place 69 Guestrow (Shooting
    Saloon)
Still's Court 18 Castle Street
Still's Court 88 Shiprow
Sutherland's Court 20 James Street
Sutherland's Court 126 Gallowgate
Sutherland's Court 78 Shiprow
Thom's Court 67 High Street
Thom's Place 63 High Street
Thomson's Court 69 West North Street
Thomson's Court 61 Broad Street
Thomson's Court 21 Quay
Thornton's Court 29 Guestrow & 4
    Flourmill Brae.
Tytler's Court 69 The Green
Victoria Court 54 Castle Street
Walker's Court 37 Shiprow
Walker's Court 61 Guestrow
Walker's Court 37 College Street
Walker's Court 30 Virginia Street
Watt's Court 111 Gallowgate
Watt's Court 28 Virginia Street
Watson's Court 45 North Street
Webster's Court 72 Shiprow
Webster's Court 2 Guestrow
Webster's Court 19 East North Street
Well Court 14 Broad Street
West Court 32 Guestrow
Wilson's Court 91 Broad Street
Winlaw's Court 107 Gallowgate
Wrights and Coopers Place 82 High Street
Yeat's Court 30 Netherkirkgate

'The Toon had then but ten short streets; to ilka hoose there wis a yaird. But these auld yairds grew sturdy reets, an' ilka gate had aye its gaird.'

Some courts were sketched or photographed, because of their ancient looking tower houses—'cleanlie and beautiful, neat both within and without. Most of them were four storeys high (some of them higher), slated and built of stone,' wrote Parson Gordon.

After 1745, the ancient back garden ground was built over, and congestion occurred in these 'pends'. The introduction of the Police Act in 1795 meant that there was systematic naming and numbering of streets and courts. Some of the closes bear the personal names of feuars or proprietors, and this is an aid for those tracing their family history.

St. Paul's, Gallowgate seen through the arch (1721) (Loanhead Granite). The original Episcopal Chapel (1721–1865), attended by Lord Byron and his mother when they stayed in Broad Street, has been rebuilt.

Some sayings in the Granite trade

'A hert o' granite and heid o' melon.'

A doctor, an undertaker and a granite mason standing in a bar: The doctor, 'I bring them into the world.' Undertaker, 'I bury them.' Mason reflects . . . I pit a steen on top o' them to hud them doon.'

Concerning Marischal College:
'It's nae as big as the pyramids, but it looks better. . . . '

Upon lifting a two hundred-weight block to a wall: 'Lift it on yer knees first laddie, and the rest is easy. . . . '

Manager to apprentice: 'How are you managing?' 'Fine, here's me laying into this lump o' granite, an' it hisnae deen me ony herm. . . . ' Apprentices took a pride in the individual designs of each monument; for it was customary to throw drapery over a broken urn in the yard, so that this detail was executed differently every time.

Gilbert Gerard's House (1787) (The Girls' Hospital, Gallowgate), before its demolition c. 1905.

'The Silver City' was the work of masons who took pleasure in all aspects of detailing work. They perfected the practical side of architecture, and many of their skills have died with them. All the towers and spires in Aberdeen were either erected or re-erected in the nineteenth century, and this fact sets aside Aberdeen from provincial cities and 'provincialism'. 'The Spiral City' is not one of 'dreaming spires'. Granite components could be bought across the counter, an active encouragement for congregations who also built for themselves the best suburbs in Christendom; and so they remain today.

Those that turned to the Granite Trade in the eighteen eighties would go to America as masons during 'the coldspell', and work there. Monumental work was done in the outdoor sheds, with open fires keeping the men warm, but even so their hands froze to the shafts of their hammers.

Many veteran masons' whiskers were in danger of being singed by 'the bubbly lamp'. Before mechanisation, sand was used as the first abrasive in polishing, and masons wore moleskin trousers.

A large workforce could be heard at the different processes that involved use of the pick, puncheon, single axe and six-cut bush hammer. Emery brought out the rich natural colour of the stone to their satisfaction. Deeside Grey, Bon-Accord Black and Balmoral Red were all imported for monumental work. Quarries adjacent to the town were Loanhead, Sclattie, Auchmill, Dancing Cairns, Cairncry, Pitmuxton, Ferryhill and Craiglug. Stone from The Bay of Nigg was taken as ballast cargo to London.

☞

Rubislaw Quarry was hollowed out of a sixty foot hill. Half of Aberdeen had come out of it in two hundred years for it was 465 feet deep, 900 feet long and 750 feet wide.

GRANITE CITY STREETS

Gin it spread oot in future time,
as fast as since I wis a bairn;
there will be naught but stane an' lime
frae Rubislaw tae The Dancing Cairn.

William Cadenhead (1893)

ABBOTSFORD PLACE

Off Ferryhill Road on the east side.

An enclave of early Victorian houses that celebrate Sir Walter Scott's friendship with the Skene Family of Rubislaw House; originally there was a vista of Ferryhill House, set in its policies from the front windows.

ACADEMY STREET

From Dee Street to Crown Street

This street is named after the Bellvue Academy.

ADELPHI LANE

From Market Street to Adelphi

The City of London used to be honeycombed with passages between high buildings like Adelphi Lane, and indeed The Earl of Montrose once called Aberdeen The London of the North. (It was certainly likened to Rome, and is built on the same number of hills; Athens and its Acropolis had been a prior claim on the part of another city.) Behind the counter in nearby Patterson's Bar, the Tartan Dive, there was a ramp to the Dark Briggie, and beer barrels were rolled upwards by 'scotchboys' to their cellars.

Rubislaw Quarries, Aberdeen.

Rubislaw's 'Granite Men' and 'Muckle Steen'.

ADELPHI
From 49/51 Union Street

The Aberdeen Adelphi was laid out on the crest of St. Katherine's Hill c.1810. It is named after the three Adam Brothers who had the byename, the Adelphoi. Their father was the architect that Robert Gordon commissioned for the building which is today Robert Gordon's College. William Adam's book of precedent architectural drawings *Vitruvius Scotticus* is as important as James Gibb's *Book of Architecture*. Stone was sent by the Adam Brothers to London from Aberdeen as ballast cargo. The London Adelphi (in the vicinity of The Strand) was commenced in 1772 at a time when there was no Embankment. The great riverfront façade only lasted a century, but the vaults are reminiscent of those under Union Street.

Back in the Granite City, James Matthews, who was destined to become foremost architect of Victorian public buildings in northeast Scotland, set up an office in the Adelphi. Here he was to be seen poring over working drawings, wearing gold-rimmed spectacles and a large bow tie that added a touch of professionalism.

AFFLECK STREET
From Crown Street to the harbour

This street was named after Captain Andrew Affleck, Master Shoemaker, who was Convener of the Incorporated Trades. It seems that the Hammermen were his favourites, so he presented them with a punchbowl, giving the reason that they were the only craft that 'can mak' a guid tum'ler, an' doon it ower th' thrapple'. (The Affleck family kept a tavern in Burnett's Close, Exchequer Row, which was described as 'the most recherché eating house in the North East of Scotland'.) There can be no doubt that Captain Affleck had already learned to appreciate the company of those that could swallow a good dram of 'the cratur that would peel the bark off a granite monument'.

ALBERT STREET
From Waverley Place to Whitehall Place

Named after Queen Victoria's husband, Archibald Simpson's single- and two-storey terraces have a quite repose about them, and lead up to the United Free Church, which was opened in 1882. The architect R. G. Wilson designed it to be the cathedral for the United Presbyterian denomination, and it looks the part when viewed from the wooded howe of the Denburn.

Some of the houses date from 1851, and it was hoped that by ten years later there would be established a public park for the West End, extending as far as Fountainhall. Instead, this stretch of The Denburn became built up.

☛ Adelphi Lane.

ALBION STREET
From Park Street to Cross Street

The 'Boolgate' or the 'Bowl Road' was renamed Albion Street in 1830; so 'England' (albion) became neighbours with 'Wales'. Wales Street and Albion Street became household names when *The Daily Express* featured a 'Name The Boulevard' competition. Suggestions such as Queensway, Dee-Don Walk, Avenue Prince of Wales, Gordon Boulevard, Ian Black Highway and Glasgow Parade were among the entries. The simple title won, and today the line of Albion Street, Little Wales Street and (old) Wales Street have been incorporated into Beach Boulevard. In 1847, the year of his death, Archibald Simpson put forward a plan for a square behind the Castlehill Barracks to discourage blasts of wind from entering the city centre.

Sandcadgers bought fresh sea sand for scattering on the 'steen fleers' into town by means of donkey cart. Some of the street cries heard in this vicinity were 'San' san' fine fite san''; 'coals, coals, prime Scotch coals'; 'Wha'd buy sticks, lassies, crackin' dry? Come awa' my bonnie darlin's come an' buy.' 'Mussel Willie' sold mussels from a barrow at tuppence the coggie in the 1850s.

The lane to the public bowling green on the Links was causewayed in 1833. It was dubbed 'Satan's Seat' by the chapel folk who built The Ragged Kirk there in 1854, on the site of 'The Penny Gaff,' (an outdoor stage.) There were also 'eight low bars' in the vicinity. The space between Albion Street and Wales Street was only the width of a single tenement.

ALBYN PLACE
From Alford Place to Queen's Cross

This was an ambitious exercise in town planning by the Victorians. A Parisian-like boulevard, lined with lime trees shading the substantial villas and embellished by Queen's Cross church spire; of all the steeples which were put up in the 'Spiral City' during the nineteenth century, the design of John Bridgeford Pirie and the craftsmanship of master mason John Morgan in 1881, marks the peak of perfection in the granite trade. The three contrasting shapes of the tower and spire are deceptively simple, but the building whose detailing has been described as the most refined in the world, stands nearby; the main block of Harlaw Academy. It was formerly Mary Elmslie's Female Orphan Asylum (architect Archibald Simpson, 1840). The cube stone is free from flaws and is uniform in colour. George Walker, bookseller and friend of Washington Wilson wrote in 1886: 'There are fifty girls, orphans of married parents from the parishes of St. Nicholas, Old Machar, Nigg and Banchory-Devenick; a more happy, pleased company could hardly be seen anywhere. It is doing much good in a very quiet way, and seems to be economically and well managed.' Aberdeen society women require girls who could be trained up by this establishment to be in service because their wardrobes were becoming increasingly elaborate. In the 1860s the lady of the house chose hats from Paris, silk from China, lace from Switzerland, and wore superfine stockings that could be drawn through a finger ring. All these fol-de-rols had to be properly maintained.

ALFORD PLACE
From Union Place (Union Street) to Albyn Place

The road to the Highlands via Upper Donside. Farmers stopped at Bawbie Law's grocer's shop, where there was a good dram at the ready after a busy market day. Rubislaw Quarry workers were also in the queue.

 Albyn Place

ALLENVALE
From Riverside Drive to Hardgate

This street received its name in 1884.

The Congregational Chapel on the corner of Albion Street (1869). The parish hall was the first 'Ragged Kirk', and it required deep foundations. The foreman at the time pointed out, 'Foun' weel an' ye'll theek the better.'

ANDERSON DRIVE

From Brig o' Dee to Persley

Aberdeen's ring road—named after Sir Alexander Anderson, Lord Provost of Aberdeen, 1859–66. He was associated with many business ventures which have subsequently brought prosperity. Under his management, the city was extended over the lands of Rubislaw, Fountainhall and Morningfield.

ANGUSFIELD AVENUE

From Queen's Road to King's Gate

This district is named after Alexander Angus, bookseller, of Narrow Wynd, who improved the land during the mid eighteenth century. The moorland was cleared of boulders.

ARDARROCH ROAD

From Merkland Road East to Linksfield Road

This street has achieved world-wide fame because the Pittodrie Organ Works were situated here. The instruments were created for shipment and erection by the proprietor. The ecclesiastical authorities could also get stained glass windows made in Aberdeen. It once was a boast that most requirements of the general public could be met within the confines of the city.

ARGYLL CRESCENT

From Westburn Road to Westburn Drive

This street received its name in 1885. Its uniformly good proportion's are due to John Morgan who wanted to ensure that the view across Victoria Park from his home was not subjected to piecemeal development.

Albyn Terrace.

ASHLEY ROAD

From Great Western Road to St. Swithin Street

The original road to Friendship farm which stood on the site which the mansion house of Ashley occupies. The name is derived from Ash trees, and an expert on name derivations and old northeast sayings, May Thomson lived nearby in Ashley Gardens. In his time, G. M. Fraser the City Librarian was credited as being a fount of all knowledge for local folklore. May's public recitals of monologues and verses in the Doric language sometimes in out-of-the-way village halls made many items resurrected from the library shelves where she worked as Reference Librarian, come alive. 'Gweed folk' like her are scarce. Built to last was the Public School of 1888, designed by Jenkins and Marr. It is in the Grecian style; rustic Rubislaw ashlar window dressings with the friezes in dressed Kemnay stone.

AUCHINYELL ROAD

From Broomhill Road to Garthdee

This street is named after the Auchinyell burn, and differs from the other names in the Garthdee housing scheme which take up the names of the protagonists at the Battle of the Brig o' Dee, 1639.

Kaimhill housing, (1937) with the use of red tiles, concrete, timber and roughcasting, incorporated the idea of experimental flatted houses and cottages of entirely new design which had been under discussion for years. The requirements for the services of plasterers, bricklayers and masons was kept to a minimum.

BAKER STREET

From South Mount Street to Skene Square

The work of the Baker Incorporation in 1867, it does not have literary associations with the London street name. This may be due to Sir Arthur Conan Doyle, creator of the world's best known detective Sherlock Holmes, being an Edinburgh man. The Bakers (or Baxters)

were incorporated in 1532, and owned land at Gilcomston. In the sixteenth century everything that they made had to be sold in the open market. If this was not observed, their girdles were forfeited by the baillies who also fixed the daily prices of beef, mutton and fish. Cut-price selling was liable to fines being imposed. This was done mainly to protect them from themselves as they bid against each other for wheat.

BALTIC STREET

Prince Regent Street to the Links

A name dating from the trading days of the Prince Regent, when northeast ports handled large amounts of timber from the Baltic lands. The timber yards remain, but not places like the 'Jungle', which had a language and lore in its own right.

BANNERMILL STREET

From Cotton Street to the Links

This street, laid out in 1830, was named after the Bannermill which manufactured cotton. The factory lassies made up a song about the 'Bog Mill', as it was colloquially known. Only a fragment has survived:

> Fan I cam' by The Salmon Fishers,
> Fan I cam' by The Roperie;
> There I saw my sailor laddie,
> sailing on the raging sea.

BATH STREET

From Bridge Place to Windmill Brae

The roofline of the Royal Hotel is reminiscent of Victorian spa architecture. This was the building's first function, and the reason why the street is so named. It has nothing to do with the phrase, 'Are ye going tae th' Pooles?' To most Aberdonians it meant the theatre building nearby.

BEACONSFIELD PLACE

From Fountainhall Road to Forest Road

I wonder if Liberals have taken feus in this street; or Conservatives in Gladstone Place?

The Queen's bodyguard.

51

BEDFORD ROAD

From Powis Terrace to St. Machar Drive

The Loch burn which drains the Loch of Old Aberdeen is more interesting historically, than the name of the street.

There were stepping stones over a 'marisch' that surrounded the Bishop's Loch in Old Aberdeen. The railway cutting between Leslie Terrace and the station drained the remnants of the moss.

BELGRAVE TERRACE

From Esslemont Avenue to Craigie Loanings

This street was named by the architects Ellis & Wilson in 1884. Belgravia is the name of a fashionable quarter in London.

BELMONT STREET

From Union Street to Schoolhill

Between 1746 and the close of the eighteenth century ten new streets had been opened; amongst them, Queen Street, North Street, Virginia Street, Marischal Street, Carmelite Street, St. Andrew Street, and Belmont Street.

Belmont was the name of Portia's palace in Shakespeare's *Merchant of Venice*, and it may be no coincidence that a flight of steps down to the Denburn, which used to be navigable at this point, has merchant shipping associations with Patagonia. Patagonian Court Stairs were altered in 1807, and the stairs beside the town residence of Mr Menzies of Pitfodels, likewise in 1809, his being the principal mansion.

The street ran right through to the Green, and at it's southern end stood the Burn Kirk. This was demolished so that Union Bridge engineering works could proceed in 1802. The Congregational Church with its distinctive steeples, and the façade of the former United Free Kirk of 1869 survive however, and with St. Nicholas Church House on the corner of Gaelic Lane, make up the impressive skyline of the 'Backs of Belmont'.

To picture-goers, the 'flechie Belmont' is now part of cinema folklore. 'You got in for the price of twa jam jars'.

BERRY LANE

From Gallowgate to Loch Street

The most renowned worthy of Berry Street was Giuseppe Nardi from La Spezia in Italy, who arrived in Aberdeen over a century ago to open a fish restaurant.

BERRYDEN ROAD

From Hutcheon Street to Ashgrove Road

Berryden Road ran alongside farmland within living memory. There was always an audience of city children, eager to learn about harness, watching the Clydesdales plough. The convoy of milkcarts from the Millbank depot was also an impressive sight. The 'Co-opie' commemorated the day of the horse with a weathervane.

Berrybank was near the Kittybrewster Toll.

The Barkmill burn (an alternative name for the Westburn) crosses Berryden Road. It drove a waterwheel at Millbank. Barkmill House likewise had an entrance gate in Berryden Road. The Barkmill Asylum building of 1821 had Archibald Simpson as its architect. The obelisk which originally stood in the St. Nicholas Kirkyard was re-erected here in 1840 due to the happy associations that the institution enjoyed with John Forbes of Newe. (Castle Newe in Upper Donside was also designed by Archibald Simpson.)

BLACKFRIARS STREET

From Woolmanhill to St. Andrew Street

Where the War Memorial Lion looks pleased, and doesn't need feeding. (Outsiders can draw their own conclusions.)

In outward appearance the 'Triple Kirks' nearby, look like a derelict friary. Blackfriars itself stood in the grounds of Robert Gordon's Hospital. The Governors of Gordon's Hospital laid out this street. Blackfriars chapel of 1821 has since become a gymnasium.

Children watched country folk boarding the 'Swallow' buses at bedtime, and started to count all the domes of Aberdeen's Augustan Age, as they tried to go to sleep above the din. The Rosemount domes include Woolmanhill Hospital, the Cowdray Hall and the Central School. Once upon a time, genteel folk put brass knockers on their front doors here, but Blackfriars Street was more recently renowned for the workshops of craftsmen like 'Joiner Rae' and 'Shoemaker Tulloch'.

BLACK'S BUILDINGS

From Woolmanhill to Spa Street

Named after James Black, a winemerchant who carried on business in the lowermost building by Collie's Brig. The houses used to shake as trains approached the tunnel which was made by open excavations; the trench being covered over by a brick archway. Schoolhill Station Building of 1867 was two-storey, with an approach way from the Denburn Viaduct.

In 1831 the proprietors were ordered to pave the street 'betwixt The Wind's Eye and Black's Buildings.' Three years later the 'Wind's Eye' was eradicated.

The Gordons (C company) at the Drill Hall 1915. Notice the apron worn over the kilt.

The impressive curve of Bon-Accord Crescent is only part of an intended urban design by Archibald Simpson, who was backed by the Tailor Craft.

BLAIRTON LANE

From Broad Street to Guestrow

This street is named after the Laird of Belhelvie. The altar, pulpits and seats of the Episcopal Meeting House ended up heating the ovens in Provost Skene's House during it's occupation in the Forty-Five. The congregation have now transferred to St. John, Crown Terrace.

BLENHEIM PLACE

From Carden Place to Hamilton Place

This street was named in 1889. It is named after the palace that Sir John Vanburgh built for the Duke of Marlborough. Woodstock Road, commanding a lofty position in the old Stocket Forest, recalls the Oxfordshire town adjacent to the palace where Sir Winston Churchill was born.

Fountainhall House survives, shorn of it's avenue of trees. Dr Patrick Copland, one-time resident, invented a portable barometer to ascertain the height above sea level of the Deeside mountains, dated 1810. He was the most illustrious 'Maister o' Fountainha'.

BON-ACCORD CRESCENT

From Bon-Accord Terrace to Old Mill Road

Travellers approaching Aberdeen by stagecoach caught their first glimpse of the Granite City from Holburn Street the great road south to the Brig o'Dee. Bon-Accord Crescent is a commanding prospect set as it is on the heights overlooking the Vale of the Howeburn, and would have impressed any gentleman completing a six-day journey from London. Some folk thought that the Crescent looked like the Hanging Gardens of Babylon.

The mailguard lodged in the cottages at Bon-Accord Crescent alongside the toffs, who had a Windmill Brae man, John England, a blacksmith, make them the fine railings of 'malleable iron' which remain to this day outside their former homes. This was a street that was proud of the fact that he gave deaf and dumb children a chance in life by teaching them all he knew, without expecting the 'keys of the toun'. Then, as now, professional men welcome newcomers, considering the fact that if they 'brocht a copper into the toun, it wid be a' richt'.

BON-ACCORD SQUARE

From East to West Craibstone Streets

At Mews Cottages, coachmen lived over the dimly-lit harness rooms. The glossy horses, proudly known as Blue Blacks, were kept in readiness for late night calls. Coach houses are still a feature of the New Town. Stable hands sat up late, making up dye, blacking and harness polish. The latter was a concoction of Black Beauty boot polish, powdered resin and ordinary wax melted by the heat of a carriage lamp. When the day of the motor carriage dawned, private coachmen feared for their jobs, pointing out that 'ye canna' pit smoke an' ile on a garden'.

Outsiders who mistakenly took a short cut through the square, were frowned upon, because crinolined ladies 'took the air' in the private garden; and by an open window in East Craibstone Street, Archibald Simpson, best remembered architect of the Granite City, played airs on his violin.

Sadly, there were no fountains in the square, but Alexander MacDonald, a granite merchant, who stayed here, did supply them for Trafalgar Square.

BON-ACCORD STREET

From Union Street to Fonthill Road

Where the Post Master lived over the stableyard, which he shared with a saddler and carriage builder. The premises were redeveloped on a grandiose scale by SMT in Art Deco style, grafted on to a gable-end which retains the architectural integrity of Bon Accord Square. Campbells of Bon-Accord Street had the first motor buses, and took delivery of their first char-a-banc in 1912. They were preceded by the firm of Laing & Melvin who had built horse-drawn vehicles since 1835.

Formerly Bon-Accord Street stopped at Springbank Terrace. It was extended as far as Fonthill in 1888.

The premises at 15-19 Bon-Accord Street with the ramp for horses in the inside courtyard looks deceptively like an old coaching inn; but on closer inspection it is of concrete construction. Plans for an office and garage were completed in 1912 on behalf of James Rollo Duncan, of Tillycorthie, a mansion which he completed in the same year, using similar building materials. Mr Duncan was a self-made man and owned tin mines in Bolivia.

BRIDGE PLACE

From Bridge Street to Bath Street

This cul-de-sac was laid out on the slope behind the pantiled cottages of Windmill Brae. It is chiefly known for the Peoples' Theatre, the Palace and Poole's, Chung Ling Soo (Billy Robinson) the famous Chinese magician once appeared here with his world-famous trick of 'catching a bullet in the teeth'.

BRIDGE STREET
From Union Street to Guild Street

At the top of Bridge Street, the public buildings of the city may still jump out at the unsuspecting, yet already impressed visitor, who has caught a first glimpse of the city on arriving at the railway station. It may be this experience that prompted Thomas Hardy, an outsider to write a poem when honoured by Aberdeen University:

> I looked and thought,
>   'all it too grey and cold
> to wake my place enthusiasms of old,'
> till a voice passed
>   'behind the granite mein
> lurks the imposing beauty of a Queen.'

> I looked anew
> and saw the radient form of Her
> who soothes in stress who steers in
> storm, of the grave influence of those
> eyes sublime men count for the
> stability of time.

Bridge Street is carried on arches, and where tall buildings now stand on the west side of the street was a wooden stairway, running down in front of these boarded-up arches. On the open ground of Bridge Place

Pillar number 12 at the Brig o' Dee. The loud-speaker system could connect you with the fire brigade or the police station.

BROOMHILL ROAD
From Holburn Street to Auchinyell Road

This may appear to be just another Granite City street. In fact it originally branched off from the Hardgate, past old cottages, and became the old Braemar and Deeside Road. the broom was the thickest on the southern slopes. The 'Woodies' run from Broomhill Road at 139 to the rear of the Broomhill Avenue houses. Two cottages and one large house stood at the end of the avenue of mature trees. They have long since been, removed, but the old flintstone lane endures.

Broomhill Avenue, Terrace, and Crescent were the first five-roomed two storey semi-detached houses to be made available to private buyers at the exceptional value of £620. 'Do men leave home? Not if its a ''Modern Home''.' Newlands Crescent, Morningside Road and Gardens were likewise tempting offers for the family man from the same company.

BURNS ROAD
From Great Western Road to Cromwell Road

This street was named in 1891, the same year as saw the statue of the poet raised in Union Terrace.

BURNIEBOOZLE

The name of a mansion on the Skene road gave its name to a suburban area of Hazlehead. Walkerhillock Croft and parts of Springfield were also synoniymous with the name, which was first mentioned in 1841.

CANAL ROAD
From Causewayend to the Canal Bridge

This was the packman's track to old Aberdeen; a resting and watering place for horses. An encampment where the fires were always burning; and many a fine air was heard on the bagpipes and fiddle.

It is no wonder then, that this meeting place brought forth such a talent as Jeannie Robertson, MBE, a housewife, whose incomparable singing voice projected the ancient balladry of her lineage, and first captivated audiences saddened by the loss of Kathleen Ferrier from the concert platform in 1953.

Jeannie's cousin, Gordon Robertson (Royal Scots, now of Sydney), found different words from the public tributes, when he wrote this coronach:

> She raised the wolves of Donnachaidh
> from nadir to the zenith—
> well endowed with Burns' muse,
> scion of Celtic Kenneth (MacAlpine Mor)
> the Convenanters' sagas sang,
> of battles midst the broom;
> Virtutis Gloria Merces Domine,
> commendo Jeannie's spiritum.

CANAL TERRACE
From Virginia Street to Garvock Street

A row of three-storey houses with 'sunks' overlooking the tow path of the canal which in 1813 was unprotected. With its proximity to the Shorelands, it is not surprising that seamen, shipmasters and sawyers stayed here. It was originally called Virginia Terrace. The Canal basin was nearby. Alexander MacDonald had a pavement making yard in the vicinity during the eighteen twenties. During the previous century Colin Allan had polished granite jewelery by using fine sea sand, before iron sand was introduced.

> Neist in oor inspectin' tourie
> saw the canal frae Inverurie,
> was thocht a wonder in it's day;
> boats came by water a' the way.
> Brought grain and farm produce down
> frae Port Elphinstone to the toon;
> here to ship and in granary store.
> In Canal Basin near in Shore,
> the boats were 'livered of their load,
> some kept in toon, some sent abroad.
> Were load again wi' coals an' lime,
> to load an' 'liver took some time;
> up the canal wi' horse were towed,
> were nae wi' sails nor oars rowed,
> up through the locks didna come speed,
> some time they took to reach The Heid.
>   James Smith (1830)

(A swift boat for passengers did not come below the locks, but was moored in readiness 'a bit ayont Kittybrewster cot toun'. Two trotting horses with boys on their backs ran the sixteen miles to Port Elphinstone for 1s 6d.)

 Canal Terrace.
The Port Elphinstone Canal. 'Barefit

loons are haulin' awa' on the towpath.

Stonyton clachan, on the north side of
Carden Place between Blenheim Place
and Prince Arthur Street, 1879.

CARDEN PLACE

From Skene Street to Queen's Cross

Two contestants can fairly lay claim to having this street named after them: Saint Carden of the Cardenwells, and Jerome Carden who visited Aberdeen in 1552. Before the formation of North Albert Street, a narrow lane passed by the 'Tea Wallie', then climbed the brae to the old Fountainhall Road.

Carden Terrace of 1867 is by the local architect James Henderson. The Smiddy at 'Stonytoun' clachan shoed the heavy horses that worked at Rubislaw. The trackway between the smiddy and the cottages led to the mansion houses of Fountainhall and Whitehall which a century ago stood in open country.

CARMELITE LANE

From Hadden Street to Trinity Street

This narrow street was laid out over the Carmelite Friars garden. A bystander saw 'barrowfuls of the Carmelite Monks' bones' being taken away in a box cart during construction work in 1891. Another major dig this time by professional archaeologists in 1980 unearthed more remains. The following remedy for a headache occasioned by a hangover is culled from a collection of monks' prescriptions: 'Agains the heid aikin by muckill drinking . . . take rue levis and bray them in wynager and put royss to red and bitter almonds and wyne. Rub your heid and ye shall be eisit.'

Carmelite Buildings have been the Ironmongery empire of Cruikshank & McIntyre since the changeover from Mr Sellar in 1904.

CARMELITE STREET

From Green to Guild Street

This street was laid out in 1795. Some of the best country families originally stayed there. It was rebuilt to give an overall uniform appearance by the Victorians.

CAROLINE PLACE

From Skene Square to Hutcheon Street

Teams up with Charlotte Street, also in the Lochlands. Queen Caroline and George III were crowned on 22 September 1761. The occasion was ushered in by the ringing of bells and blazing of bonfires; a concert was held in Marischal College; the healths of the king and queen were drunk in the Castlegate amid the firing of volleys; the Trades made a grand procession through the streets and in the evening the houses were brilliantly illuminated.

The outdoor sheds where the 'granite men' worked.

The Gordons' Tailors at Castlehill Barracks.

Corporation Electric Works Smiddy.

CASTLE TERRACE
From Castle Street to Fish Street

Castle Terrace is chiefly remembered for the Sick Children's Hospital of 1877. It later became Cocky Hunter's Bargain Store. The stair to Castle Brae from Cowgate was removed in 1839. On the slopes of Castlehill were the kailyards where curly kail and cabbage were grown. Custocks and runts stalks of kail were renowned for their juicy sweetness in broth. Sometimes it was the only food taken during fasting periods.

Cauld kail in Aberdeen
and custocks in Strathbogie;
and yet I fear they'll cook o'er soon,
and ne'er warm the cogie.

> Cocky Hunter's Bargain Store, Castle Terrace.
> 'If ye want a knocker for your door
>   or a hoose tae fit yer fleer.
> Ging tae Cocky Hunter's Store in
>   Aiberdeen.'

Cocky Hunter's store was 'itself a hub of Commerce'. The family prided themselves on selling anything from a needle to an anchor.

CATHERINE STREET
From George Street to Causewayend

This street was laid out 1806–7 but not extended until it was paved in 1828. It was possible to 'big an' furnish a hale hoose' in the length of this street. If hard times came, there was also a pawnbroker's to turn to. James Nicol at the Vulcan Works (No 18) was a blacksmith. In addition to this, he made toe plates for walking boots; small, medium, and large ladies' heel and toe plates.

☛ Vulcan Works Catherine Street.

COLLEGE STREET AND SOUTH COLLEGE STREET

From Windmill Brae to Wellington Bridge

Dominated by the railway arches. The first viaduct was constructed of brick in 1848, but was replaced with granite in 1904.

Under the arches, family businesses established themselves, and brewery drays set out from here to deliver Black's beer from Devanha brewery to local bars.

The old warehouse was remarkable for The King and Queen posts with accompanying 'jack' in its roof. Originally the extent of College Street was from Windmill Brae to Affleck Street and this section was paved in 1829. Women who worked in Pirie's factory putting black borders on notepaper and envelopes were dubbed 'paper angels'.

COMMERCE STREET

From Regent Quay to Justice Street East North Street and Park Street

Constructed in 1760, as part of the Shorelands improvement on land belonging to the Bowie Well Croft. In fact a pig sty was removed as late as 1835. The Mariner's Kirk stood on the site of the Bennico Centre. It was said of the congregation:

What brocht this kirk tae ruin—drinkin'!
What were the ither kirks deein' . . . winkin'!
A cast-iron bridge linked the Barracks. Barracks Hospital. The latter was a three-floored edifice with fine proportions.

CONSTITUTION STREET

From 'the Park Road, across the Aberdeenshire Canal to the Links'

Built in 1807 as Park Place, over Fill the Cap Croft, at the north side of the Castlehill. The croft was so named because of the caps on the heads of criminals on display at the Justice Port. Upon George III's refusing to politically emancipate the Roman Catholics it was swiftly changed to Constitution Street to uphold the King's decision 'to support our happy constitution'. Another proposal to call it Denmark Street was submitted in 1818. It is rather ironic that St. Peter's Roman Catholic School (now the Shiprow Tavern) was admitted after all the political fuss, but much good work was done amongst poor families in the east end.

Alexander MacDonald, founder of the monumental granite industry made paving stones, chimney pieces and gravestones at his works. He was motivated when he happened to see examples of polished granite from Egypt. He was commissioned by Royalty to make a memorial seat for John Brown and he made Napoleon III's sarcophagus. He also sculpted the Granite Duke to be enjoyed by the citizens of Aberdeen. It was transported to the Castlegate by horsepower. His works later became Ross's scrapyard, but this was in the era of the trams that passed this way.

Barrel Doddie lived in South Constitution Street around the 1920s. He bought 'a' kinds o' boxies an' barrels' which he cleaned and repaired then re-sold.

Weighbridge at Ross's yard Constitution Street. The former granite yard offices can be seen in the background. Over three hundred men were employed in its hey day.

COTTON STREET

From Miller Street to Links Road

Where salmon workers and weatherbeaten men who took their stallions around the farms in the summer, found work in the winter. Gas works wages were not high, because there was plenty of labour to be found elsewhere.

Cotton Street was home for railway guards and foremen who worked at Waterloo Station. Schoolchildren who used the playing field on the links thought that the 'shoppie' here sold the finest penny drinks. On the way back to Hanover Street and more lessons, they marvelled at the heavy men and heavy horses of the shore porters workforce. Bairns came down here with prams to buy coal and cinders, but found a few that had fallen out of the gasworks engine cab: 'Paddy at the railway picking up steens—along came an engine and knocked Paddy's beens. "Oh", said Paddy, "that's na fair", "Oh", said the engine man, "ye shouldnae be there".'

The old 'Cake Mill' where cattle cake was manufactured. The North East Agricultural Coop's premises at Bannermill seen from the G.N.S.R. sidings looking towards Constitution street, the sidings have since been built upon.

Bannermill Place was a new street from Bannermill Road at Cross Street. The North East Agricultural Co-operative Society extended the Mills. The level of Bannermill Road was raised when it became part of Beach Boulevard.

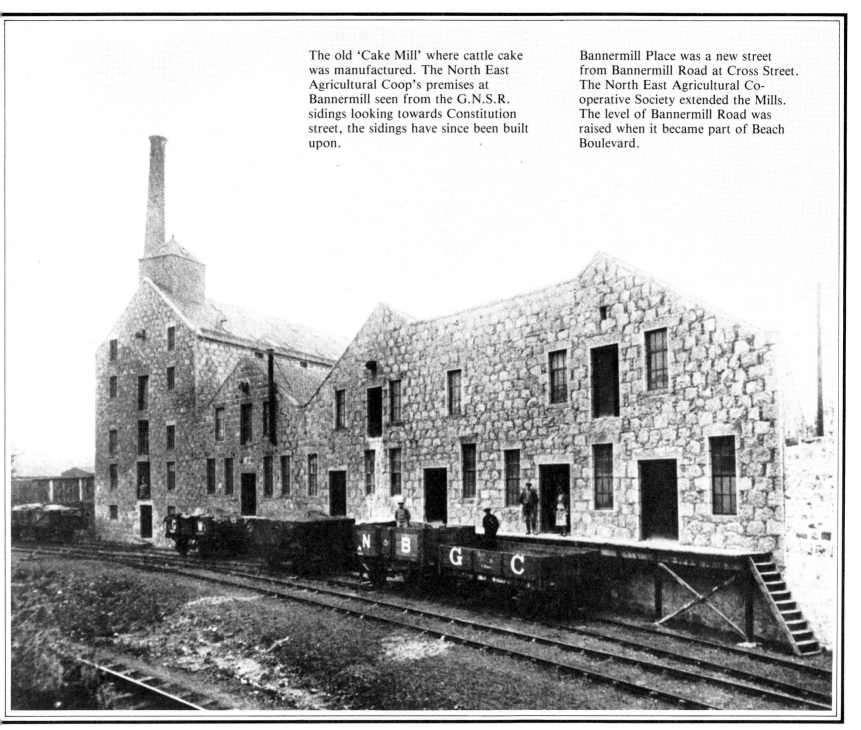

Church Street. 👆

The distinction between North Charlotte Street and South Charlotte Street was dropped in 1893. The southern end was the oldest, it's curbstones getting a mention in 1805.

CHRONICLE LANE
From North Street to Mealmarket Street

Named after the *Aberdeen Chronicle*. This newspaper went defunct in 1832.

CHURCH STREET
From Waterloo Street to St. Clement Street

The site of the old village of Footdee was cleared in 1808 and rebuilt as the fisher squares further east. Church Street leading to the church of St. Clement was ordered to be paved in 1831. There were town planning schemes afoot for the area at the time but they were subsequently dropped.

👈 Chapel Street.

CIRCUMBENDIBUS

A railway line which was to have run from Woodside, via Stockethill, Queen's Cross and Albyn Place to Guild Street.

In 1866, when the railway from the south was being extended to Aberdeen, the engineers found difficulty in blasting their way through rocks at Muchalls. A plan was prepared to take the line in a sweep from Stonehaven round by Ardoe, entering the city via Osborne Place.

CLARENCE STREET

From Church Street to Wellington Street

This street is named after the Duke of Clarence who was similarly honoured in shipyard districts of other cities. Foot pavements were laid down in 1838. Clarence Street and Lime Street were the site of Old Fittie village,

A beer label from Black's Devanha Brewery.

The Charlotte Bar.

The workforce of J. J. Ingram.

CAUSEWAYEND

From Gallowgate to Powis Place and Gowan Brae

A lean street, where many children died in the depression years.

Poets have written about the slaty greyness of the Powis Place district, and the cutting weather there on November nights, This was a place where even young women wore dark shawls. Their little houses have been swept away, although a meeting place, a coffin-shaped building known as the Coffiny, with it's summer seat remained until 1983 as a reminder of the old days. Peter Herkless kept a menagerie here. It consisted of mice, cats, dogs, ferrets, squirrels, larks, a hawk, a fox and a mangy wolf.

The street was named after the Calsey Croft, and was ordered to be paved in 1839. The calsay makers used 'a reel' to finish the setts roughly. Fine dressed setts were also produced. J. J. Ingram moved in 1898 from Causewayend to 72 Hutcheon Street. The workforce were sorry to move, because their previous premises were next to Bendelow's pie shop where the pie cost a penny farthing and an eighteen-inch apple tart cost 1s.

CHAPEL LANE

From Weigh House Square to Shore Brae

This street was named after a room set aside in a warehouse for purposes of worship. The byeway was liable to flooding and was paved in 1830 to help drainage. Chapel Lane is one of the lost streets of Aberdeen, but it does not deserve to be forgotten.

Stonemason to apprentice:
'If I had a farthing for every ton of granite used for building Aberdeen, I could buy the other half of the world.'

CHAPEL STREET

From Union Street at Union Place to Skene Street

This street is mentioned in connection with its pavements in 1832, and the removal of a public pump. Today it is cut short at Huntly Street and has assumed a Little Chelsea atmosphere. the chapel referred to was the one attached to, the Bridewell Prison. In the minds of exiles this street stands out for its 'potted heid' and fish and chips.

CHARLOTTE STREET

From St. Andrews Street to Maberley Street

Queen Charlotte was respected by Aberdeen. This street runs the complete length of the former loch, and bears her name, but folk knew the place better as being the home of Mutter Howie railway contractors. Carters competed for the best turn out, and well-groomed horses that liked 'butter bars', stood twenty hands high. Matched pairs of hearse horses were stabled here, making daily trips to where they were required.

It's a life, it's a life;
It's a weary, weary life.
It's baitter tae be single
than tae hae a married wife.

One says, 'Marmie,
gie us a piece an' jam';
The ither says, 'Deddie,
gie us a hurlie in a pram.'

CRAIGIE STREET
From George Street to Charlotte Street

This was one of the new streets laid across the Lochlands. This portion was drained by 1853, when the first tenements were erected. Bairns lying in bed of a morning heard Mutter Howie's horses plodding by, and noticed that the heavy Clydesdales trotted homeward in the evening knowing where they were going after a hard day's work. In the evenings there were impromptu concerts in the 'backies' featuring roller skating, tap dancing, singing, and sometimes the mandolin was played to the tea-supping audience up until midnight. Harry Johnston, who stayed at number 20 Craigie Street devised a permutation for Thomas Strang's football coupons. His daughter, Pearl Stewart who has made antique jewellery her business, writes about the high days and holidays in a typical tenement street:

Yesterday in Craigie Street
Tar, the smell o' it—'the tarry biler'
  reekin' . . .
Hot summers melting bubbles in the cobbles
  of yesterday—
I, barefoot—prancing—dancing—
Black lumps o't on my bonnie frock, bought
  on a Friday
at 'The Castler'. I mind it fine; a real prood
  quine,
and it only cost 'a tanner'.
Ah yesterday . . . easy paces, friendly
  faces . . .
Far are they a' the day?

Cotton Street.

Cinder wives from Cotton Street.

70

CROOKED LANE
From St. Andrew Street to Loch Street

Laid out on the banks of the former Loch. Carters and coal dealers had their stores here. The Oddfellows, a small bar here only accommodated a few folk, including boys who took lemonade. 'The toilet only held half a man.' Frater's bookie shop and the public baths were other 'weel-kent' establishments. There was a Crooked Lane by London Bridge, but the Aberdeen street name perpetuates the name Crooked Myres.

'The Coalmannie'.

Na, yesterday in Craigie Street fowk wid get the gither,
gang picnics tae The Bay o' Nigg, a whale busload a tenement.
Lang summer holidays; sweet content . . .
Primus stoves an' kettles; tatties tae bile . . . hard-biled eggs.
We'd a' pick buckies, gither delse; were they 'The Good old Days'
or were they something else?
Yesterday was Bendylow's pies and 'fatty bannocks'; 'Lucky Tatties'
Trainy Parkie, Wordie's horses . . . thoughts provoke
Aye happy days—nae discontent; jist hard workin' fowk in a tenement.

 Craigie Street looking towards The Grand Central Cinema in George Street.

Aberdeen Picture Palaces, who owned The Capitol, Playhouse, Star, Kings and The Globe, opened a cinema which provided seats for 2500. No seat was dearer than a shilling. It was known as the City Cinema.

CRAIGIEBUCKLER

Originally part of the Muir of Pitfodels.

THE GENERAL POST OFFICE, ABERDEEN.

CRAIGIE LOANINGS, ROSEMOUNT

From Albert Street and Whitehall Place to Rosemount Place

A lane named after a fifteenth-century burgess, Alexander Crag.

Loanhead village stood at the head of this loaning. Quarry workers lived there, and occasionally beggars who were not permitted to settle in the town. The quarry 'pinnan' hill has been unearthed during the completion of suburban villas. Stone for Robert Gordon's College, Gilcomston Chapel plus most of the older fabric of Gallowgate and Broad Street came from here by the mid eighteenth century.

CROWN STREET

From Union Street to Ferryhill Road

Although this is one of the oldest Granite City streets (it was all built by 1828), the chief architectural glories came much later. Instead of Crown Place, there stands a tower house castle (The Post Office) (1906). Trinity Congregational Chapel is a lesser known work of James Matthews (1876–8). James Sottar designed the Methodist and Baptist chapels in Crown Terrace. The Masonic Temple is unique and awe-inspiring. It has the hallmark of a James Gibbs design. It is one of the city's celebrated understatements that the eminent architect was 'a Fittie loon forgotten'. The portrait studio used by the photographer George Washington Wilson, made way for an imposing office building, in which the Etching King James McBey had a small studio before he left Aberdeen. The Star and Garter building is tall, so the Windmill Brae is the best vantage point to see how this corner embellishes Crown Street, and gives the place an air of importance.

Masonic Temple, Crown Street.

CUPARSTONE LANE
From Great Western Road to Ashvale Place

The name derives from the names cooper and caupmaker. There is a similar name, Capraston, which preceded the name Hilton. Balneaves the blacksmith repaired 'hurley' wheels, one of the last to do so.

DEE STREET
From Union Street to Dee Place

This originally was Upper Dee Street. Lower Dee Street, nearer the Denburn, was an older thoroughfare; it ran from Trinity Street to The Lower Denburn; it received its name 'by some accident unknown to the Police Commissioners' in 1809.

The layout of Dee Street and neighbouring Gordon Street is disjointed due to a cluster of pantiled property formerly existing along Old Mill Road.

The Jewish Synagogue is in a terrace house, and the Aberdeen Jews are buried in The Grove Cemetery. Moses Scialitti, a Florentine Jew was the first-mentioned merchant to represent the Chosen People, that was recorded in Aberdeen (1669).

An outsize inscription shows that Mary Garden, world-famous opera singer was born in this street. The platter format is appropriate because a Chicago restauranteur honoured her by giving pride of place on his sweet trolley to Meringue Mary Garden. Upon being informed of this culinary homage she remarked that she 'would rather be remembered that way than forgotten.'

Laying tramlines in Crown Street. The street still suffers from the fact that it has a curve. This was necessary otherwise Windmill Brae would have had to have been bridged by Union Street.

Dee Village Square looking towards
South Crown Street. The brick-built
cottages were demolished in 1898 to
make way for The Aberdeen Electricity
works.

Oot by Dee Village wha' oor thirst
at its wee well we'd slake,
aye mindin' still tae leave a preen
for ilka drink we'd tak'

Wiliam Cadenhead

The Denburn viaduct, *c.*1888. Oxen transported the white granite ex Mr Fyfe's quarry at Kemnay, which was also a source for many of the cassies seen about the city. Blue granite came from Manuelle's quarry at Dyce. The panels are in pink Correnie granite. Beyond the Denburn Road arch can be seen Black's Buildings. Many of the bridge builders carried milk cans with lids on them to work, so that they could have a drink with their 'piece'.

DEE VILLAGE SQUARE

Off South Crown Street

The old Dee Village was demolished in 1822 by Captain Dingwall Fordyce, an advocate. The Planned Village Square which he built in local brick could easily fit into the Norfolk landscape; an Aberdeen Akenfield. The Potter's Creek, a quay from where the pantiles, that glowed in the sunset, (and the bricks likewise), were loaded aboard ship. The Ferryhill burn drove Provost George Auldjo's pottery wheel. His flowerpots, chimney pots, domestic ware (black and brown) and the distinctive 'tortoiseshell' decorative pieces.

DENBURN ROAD

From The Green to Woolmanhill

A fleeting trail of white granite dust was left by the heavy wheels of the horse lorries, that left worn furrows by the kerbside, as they braked sharply on the steep descent into a vibrating labyrinth.

The cassies were continually being worn down by cabs and two-wheeled milk carts, because the horses and carriers worked from four in the morning until seven at night.

Denburn Road improvments provided employment during 1884 and 1885 for labourers. It was a time of expansion for it is contemporary with the Shorelands and Riverside Road engineering works.

'Parcel Sandy' who laboured for Walker's Parcel Express on the Peterculter run, fed and harnessed his own horses. Town horses slept in moss litter, and it was regular work to cog the horses shoes in the morning with strips of metal from syrup tins. He soon told the blacksmith, if he gave him cheek, that 'yer cogholes are like yer mou'; too big, an' in the wrang place.' Another repartee was, 'Chappie, the wheels may be roun' but the shafts are gey licht.' Sandy worked late into his seventies, and never acquired a cart without bargaining for the rope to hold on the load. Leather-helmeted loons playing on the bucket swings in the Denburn Road Playground by the Trainie Park, thought that he looked like a weatherbeaten old Red Indian.

An engraving of Union Brig (1805) under construction. The engineer in charge was Thomas Fletcher.

ABERDEEN BRIDGE.

Courtesy of Leopard Magazine

DESSWOOD PLACE
From Whitehall Place to Forest Road

This formed the western end of the old Fountainhall Road which ran westward from Short Loanings. Lined with Ontario poplars it is named after Alexander Davidson of Desswood who resided up The Deeside. He was chairman of The Aberdeen Land Association. The fountain, which is now at the southern perimeter of Duthie Park was one of six cisterns in the locality.

The tattie pickers, setting off for Kincorth from the Denburn Road depot. A hard day's work lay ahead for these bairns, who 'grafted' like adults from a very early age.

DEVANHA TERRACE
From South Crown Street to Prospect Terrace

An impressive terrace overlooks the Dee (this is the neo-Roman version of the name).

Aberdeen's only two storey 'but and ben', 1½ Devanha Terrace, is a rural reminder of the Deeside Railway, built in 1853 and closed, 1966.

Provost Henderson lived at Devanha House (1840) and his hot house blooms were famous before Duthie Park's greenhouses. Devanha Place and Gardens have sprung up in the grounds of this Tuscan villa.

DIAMOND STREET
From Union Street to North Silver Street

This street name is the most valuable-sounding amongst a group containing also Ruby and Silver. Golden Square is the best known portion of a larger plan to have linked squares on the northern side of Union Street. This grandeur did not materialise and instead Diamond Street became a mecca for the horse hirer and funeral undertaker. Campbell's cabbies were used to 'calling, and standing' in readiness.

The house with the pillars, (later The Royal Bank), was the town residence facing on to Union Street of James Hadden of Persley. The Diamond Merchant's House however has been pulled down.

DRUM'S LANE
From Upperkirkgate to Loch Street

This thoroughfare was paved *c*.1800, and took in some of the garden ground beside Lady Drum's Hospital (almshouses) where widows and 'old indigent virgins' bade. There was an application in 1843 to lay wooden paving, but this was refused. Drum's Lane had its own school at the south end, kept by John Ross at the time the youthful Byron attended it in 1794. At the other end of the street latterly stood the Psychic Centre.

With the recent clearances, a view of the Loch Kirk, behind the shop frontage at no. 52/58 George Street, has been opened up.

EDEN PLACE
Off Rosemount Place

This street is built over nursery grounds. It is first mentioned in the directories for 1870. East of this cul-de-sac lies Short Loanings, which in the 'forties and 'fifties was renowned for it's dilapidated dwellings; and it was dangerous to walk there alone at night. The Garden of Eden or The Land of Nod?

ELMBANK TERRACE
From Canal Road to Bedford Road

Rather select villas were built along the bank of the Aberdeenshire canal. The dark thickets of the Powis Estate, with it's secluded mansion house on the distant ridge, and the pool of fishes after which it was named, made this, in comparison, the sunnyside.

At 16 Elmbank Road, the music composer Ronald Center was born on 2 April 1913. His compositions are now more often performed outside Aberdeen. Fervid and throbbing, the message he conveys, hints at the depths of northeast consciousness.

The old fountain cistern, through which the city's water supply was piped. Whitehall can be seen far right, *c*.1900.

ESSLEMONT AVENUE
From Skene Street to Rosemount Place

The most memorable of all tenement streets. It was commenced in the 1880s. Forrester's Buildings on the corner of Leadside Road have the date 1895 indelibly cut in stone. Rosemount School is by the architect James Souttar and is suitably ponderous. The West-field wing of the Grammar School is neo-gothic with matching wooden tracery in the windows. The Grammar School is blithely baronial.

EVENINGFIELD

There is no land in Rubislaw with a western exposure to warrant the name Eveningfield. The name actually refers to a gardener's cottage. It is a subtle bit of place naming even if it looks diminutive beside Morningfield.

EXCHANGE STREET
From Hadden Street to Guild Street

Named after the Corn Exchange. The Catholic apostolic church has become a fruit store. Trinity Church, later the Alhambra Music Hall, has also survived.

Jolly Boy's Picnic

FARMER'S HALL
From Baker Street to Rosemount Place

The name has its origins in the 1760s when a large barn for storing malt was built.

FARRIER LANE
From West North Street to Mealmarket Street

Peter Forrest the horse shoer was at hand for the carriers' horses.

FERRYHILL PLACE
From Fonthill Road to Marine Place

In the 1853/4 Street Directory four ship-masters resided here.

FISH STREET
From the Tarry Brig to Albion Street

The masons who built the world-famous Gothic cathedrals of Europe would not have been ashamed of the craftsmanship of West St. Clement's church. Their masterpieces will be admired for ever, but West St. Clement's is gone.

Macaulay's Riddle
(Mr Macaulay, Inspector of stamps, stayed in Crown Street.)
Cut aff my heid, hoo singular I act:
Cut aff my tail, and plural I appear.
Cut aff my heid an' tail must curious fact
altho' my riddles left, there's naething there.
What is my heid aff? a sounding sea.
What is my tail cut off? a flowing river.
  Amid its mingling depths I fearless play
  parent of softest sounds, the mute forever.
(A cod fish in the River Dee)

Elmbank Terrace.

FONTHILL ROAD

From Ferryhill Place to Holburn Street

The street was originally named St. Machar Road, but in 1892 was changed. Fonthill house, occupying a commanding position between Albury Road and Ferryhill House was built by Harvey Hall who had connections with the Farquhars of Fonthill Abbey, former home of the eccentric collector, William Beckford. Thus Fonthill Road is named after a famous gothic folly, and an Aberdeen granite villa.

Fountainhall looking north.

Tram depot Fountainhall Road.

FORBES STREET

From Rosemount Place to Rosemount Terrace

James Staats Forbes was paid ten thousand pounds for 'the marrisch and miring feus of The Lochlands'. There was a Lochlands Tontine, 1815–30.

FOREST AVENUE

From Great Western Road to Forest Road

In 1896 the name was changed from Forest Road South.

FOREST ROAD

From Forest Avenue to South Stocket Road (King's Gate)

Sir Alexander Anderson wished the historic associations of the old Stocket forest to be thus preserved.

Houses in Forest Avenue, Forest Road, Ferryhill Road and Queen's Road were made available by Modern Homes (Aberdeen) Limited at prices starting from £950.

FOUNTAINHALL ROAD

From Queen's Cross to Beechgrove

On Fountain Hall Road Corner a relay of horses awaited their horse-drawn tram and worked a four-hour shift. The name Fountainhall refers to the mansion in Blenheim Place, but a 'fountain haugh' also means a hollow.

The skating pond here was also a popular rendez-vous. This street, with its delightfully proportioned villas was laid out in 1876.

FREDERICK STREET
From King Street to Park Street

This street was where the horse-drawn steam pumping engine was housed. The Fire Master also did duty as Lighting Inspector. Those part-time officers under him such as chimney sweeps and slaters were rounded up by a messenger. This had to be done before they could attend to a fire. A bad fire in Marischal Street was a disaster that led to the reorganisation of the fire brigade.

The Frederick Street public school changed the skyline of this quarter of the city when it opened in 1905. Originally it could take 332 infants and 764 senior/junior pupils. The rooftop playground measured 750 square yards, children skipped to their favourite games like 'caw caw the ropie', and when playing with a ball they would sing, 'One, two, three a leerie, I spied Bella Peerie.' Some sang and played the Grand old Duke of York, The farmer in the dell, In and out the dusty bluebells, and Ring a ring o' roses.

Frederick Street School's rooftop playground. On the opposite side of the street was Shuttle Lane School, where charity dinners were held in the festive season, when 'Mr Ledingham the baker gave 500 lb of plum pudding for the delectation of waifs'.

GAELIC LANE

From Belmont Street to Back Wynd

The 1795 shell of the chapel built for the Gaelic-speaking congregation of Aberdeen still stands. St. Columba's Dee Street (now Gabriels) was used subsequently. The bath house at the foot of Patagonian Stairs nearby was also a meeting place for the Gaels, and the name 'Patagonian' is a phonetic variant of the old gaelic for 'bath house.' This disclosure doesn't dismiss the possibility of trading links with Patagonia either.

Aberdonians were tolerant towards the Gaelic congregation, and did not shun their language or culture.

GARDEN'S LANE

From Justice Street to East North Street

Not to be confused with Gardner's Lane off West North Street. These were fever-infested 'backies'; part of the city's past which should remain buried, but not forgotten.

GAS STREET

From Trinity Street to Poynernook

This street was paved in 1833. Gas was sold privately by Gassy Gordon.

George Street

GEORGE STREET ☞

From St. Nicholas Street to Powis Terrace

This street is named after George III, but it is not lined all the way to 'Split The Win' with stately edifices and public buildings. The section from St. Nicholas Street commenced life as Tannery Street and was paved as far as St. Andrew Street by 1802. The 'Loch Kirk' belongs to this era. It is hidden behind a modern shop frontage at 52/58 George Street; the 'body of the kirk' forming an upstairs showroom. This was the first church building to be lit by a gasolier (made by Allan & Simpson for Convener Affleck), a member of this secession kirk (1826) (the oldest united Presbyterian kirk). Its courtyard has disappeared and its southern façade is masked by a modern building. The Unitarian Chapel on the corner of Maberly Street (1840), has been replaced by garage showrooms, and the Church of Scotland Training College for Teachers now stands derelict.

'Splitties' was a bar where carriers needed 'a whet' when it was dry, and were dry when it was wet. The windswept corner is presently occupied by A. Marshall Mackenzie's kirk (1895) in the pre-reformation style of Old Greyfriars, Broad Street. It was originally intended that a spire and transepts should be added. Archibald Courage who had a shop at 7 George Street no doubt supplied the academic texts for Marischal College. The place was low-roofed and two steps down from street level. The proprietor was most attentive and wore a deep-folded gingham neckerchief which was tied wayfaring-style twice around the neck.

Local children looked forward to the annual Jolly Boys Drive. It was organised by the Westside Dairy, whose Jubilee Milk won a silver teapot at the Kittybrewser Show.

Clark & Rose's fleet of removal vehicles. The cemetery cottage was ☞ rebuilt at the top of Rubislaw Den South.

GERRARD STREET

From Gallowgate to George Street.

Named after a minister of Greyfriars' Professor Alexander Gerrard, a professor of theology at the old Marischal College, who died in 1795.

His essays on genius and taste attracted the attention of Immanuel Kant, whose grandfather was a native of Aberdeenshire.

Today, the tenements where the Broadford Mill lassies stayed have been replaced by high rise flats. 'The shoppie with its little entrance bell' where they got their messages, has gone, leaving the Kirk with its moorish minarets in splendid isolation.

GOLDEN SQUARE

From South Silver Street to North Silver Street

Where delivery boys tip-toed down basement stairs to pay their first call at the kitchens of stately granite town houses, carrying hooped baskets covered with a white cloth.

Below stairs, weatherbeaten bobbies on the evening beat supped strong tea out of bowls in the housekeeper's room and ate her scones, while their outsize bicycle saddles soaked up the dew against the railings.

Many people associated Union Place as being the quarter in town where the doctors resided. Many, however, preferred Golden Square. Dr William Sinclair who resided at 20 Golden Square also owned the Lands of Altens, Loirston, Doonies and Kirkhill.

GORDON STREET

Off Langstane Place

This street was the work of Thomas Gordon, mason, whose son founded the firm of Gordon & Smith in Union Street. A line of poplars was a feature of the New Town of Aberdeen as it advanced in a southerly direction.

GREAT SOUTHERN ROAD

From Holburn Street to Kincorth

This alternative approach road from the south was built over the Fonthill rubbish tip and opened in 1938.

Servants wearing freshly laundered aprons gave them a piece of fruit or shortbread, because housekeepers relied on tradesmen 'By Royal Appointment' in their daily planning, to do 'impossibilities straight away', even if 'miracles might take a little longer'. Next it was the turn of the window cleaners who saw that the long sash windows gleamed every day. Wooden slatted venetian blinds were cleaned with a fine brickdust paste.

Hutcheon Street Corner.

The statue of George, the fifth and last Duke of Gordon was set up in the square in 1952. It was designed by Thomas Campbell and sculpted in Dancing Cairns granite (1841–2). It was one of the first statues to be cut in granite since the Ptolemies. With Silver Street on either side Golden Square can still be described as 'an apple of Gold in a basket of Silver'.

GREAT WESTERN ROAD

From Nellfield Cemetery to the Waterworks

Covent Garden market porters thought that Robert Balmanno's plants yielded the finest crop of strawberries in Great Britain, during the eighteenth century.

The 'Manno' field Enclosures that he farmed as strawberry fields were in the vicinity of present-day Cromwell and Countesswells Roads.

The new street names give an impression that this is the City's French Quarter, with its chic 'Villes' and 'Places'.

Much of the building work proceeded in Brighton Place, Grove Street, Braemar Place and Allan Street in the 1880s. Forty years earlier, the lands of Pitmuxton lay beyond the police boundaries.

Near Pitmuxton House which stood between Salisbury Terrace and Pitstruan Place until 1904 was the Rock of Collielaw. It was quarried away. The Northern Brick and Tile Works was also at Pitmuxton.

GUILD STREET
From Market Street to Bridge Street

Named after Dr Guild who purchased the monastery and chapel of Trinity Friars and gave it to the incorporated trades to be a meeting house and hospital (1633).

The street was laid out in 1854 and teenage tracer boys were employed to guide the heavy loads up Marischal, Market and Bridge Streets. They frequented Guild Street when business was slack, making sure that a 'mou-bag' weight dangled from the horse's collar, thus preventing the wooden-bottomed canvas from knocking passers-by. A perquisite of the job was the end product, which sold for a penny a bucket.

The Station yard often was the place where new arrivals were photographed; Washington Wilson, whose firm was kept busy recording the new locations of statues as the corporation had them moved to the bewilderment of visitors; gave one of the carillon bells from Louvain, to the Town.

In 1857, Fiddler's Wallie was presented to 'the inhabitants of the world' by Sandy Fiddler, a dealer in 'coalies' by the quay. The watch that was given as a token of appreciation cost £20, and to the amusement of Aberdonians, the well only cost £18. Rudyard Kipling wrote a poem that would have pleased Mr Fiddler; it began:

> The beasts are very wise,
> their mouths are clean of lies.

The Station yard; ex glass plate negative.

Guild Street, Aberdeen

Her Majesty's Theatre and Opera House (1872) later known as the Tivoli.

HADDEN STREET
From Market Street to Carmelite Street

Named after James Hadden, Lord Provost 1801–31, known as the Father of the City—because due to his foresight Union and King streets were laid out, and the improvement to the harbour by Thomas Telford realised.

Hadden's woollen mill. dominated the south end of the Green. It was the first to introduce improved hosiery machinery, by Arkwright. 'Country loons looking for a 'fee', a brown paper parcel under their arm, stood in wait looking for employers who wore large gold watch chains. The corn exchange depot was where bargains were struck with a dram, and a slap of the hand.'

Horse parades were held here with patent leather and silver buckles. Remarks were overheard: 'It's a lot o' flash, but the tails hae richt tied up.'

After the horsedealing was over, women were present in and around the bars. . . .

HAMILTON PLACE
From Craigie Loanings to Forest Road

A punchbowl of architectural styles ranging from lobbies shaped like horseshoes to spirelet rooms, where families who could afford a telescope trained it on the stars and the neighbours.

At the west end of Hamilton Place which was extended in 1898, past the southern front of Honeybrae farm where Lord Byron spent a summer of his youth, lived an east end worthy, the dancing master Francis Peacock, who eloquently called his country retreat, the Villa Franca. One successful tradesman tried to buy respectability when he built an imposing retirement home in granite, but found that to the toonsfolk he was still 'the snuff dealer that bides at Sneezin' Ha''.

The street is named after a professor who built an observatory on the Castlehill, and it was laid out c.1888.

Professor Robert Hamilton also wrote a book on *The National Debt* (1813). This gave him a European reputation at the time. Aberdeen just knew him as an absent-minded academic. One day, coming out of college he walked up against a cow, and humbly apologised; but a short time after, he stumbled against a lady and exclaimed, 'Are you there again, you brute?' Another day, whilst deeply immersed in some problem he walked into the canal; upon which a passing wifie held up her hand and commented: 'A' weel . . . they hae muckle tae answer for; at last ye gang yer lane.'

HANOVER STREET
From Heading Hill to Albion Street

Named as a token of respect for the House of Hanover. On the site of Hanover Street School was an inn which was frequented by farmers. It had a deep draw well, so spring water was available for those who liked to dilute their spirits. Marie Ray's Bar and the Public Baths are also worthy of mention. The ancient Angel Well was in the vicinity of this street, as was the Angel Brae.

HARDWEIRD
Off the Upper Denburn

The burn ran open here, crossed by several bridges. Country women called to each other from opposite forestairs, as they gathered in their daily wash. Their men were often away with the Territorial Army; and the stablers nearby hired out horses when the camp was at Montrose. The lands of Hardweird were originally like a 'schangie'; rocky wasteland, and it is known that pigs were reared on this stretch of St. John's Croft.

Looking towards The Upper Denburn and Hardweird from the foot of Jack's Brae. The high wall is still in existence, but the gentleman's pissoir and the little houses of Hardweird with their forestairs are, like St. John's Croft steadings, part of the lost village of the Denburn, the 'fermtoun' within the city. Further west in Mackie Place, the eighteenth-century ogee-gabled houses are the only survivors. On the other side of the burn, a weaving shed and Cherryvale Bridge.

The Upper Denburn

Afore I could haud up my face
I'd need diurnal floodin's;
especially near the nasty place
whaur—mak's the puddin's.
But facts are chiels we mauna hide,
they're heroes e'en in oor age.
It's true upon The Hardweird side
they hinna got the sewerage . . .
They o'cht some day.

(James Ogg)

Skipping song:

My mither says I mun go
wi' my faither's dinner o'.
Chippit tatties, beef an' steak,
twa reed herrin' and a bawbie cake.

Eenery twaery, tuckery teven
hallowby crockery ten or eleven;
peem pam musky dam
feedilum fadilum twenty one.

89

The forestairs of the houses in Hardweird. At the time Washington Wilson took this picture, this part of Gilcomston was regarded as a good place to stay.

HARRIET STREET
From Schoolhill to Loch Street

Cartloads of fodder for Aberdeen's horses passed down this street. In 1853 there were five stablers here. Littlejohn's hem makers made sets of hems, 'nickel peakit' collars, and other sundries. The blacksmith obliged by putting a hot iron into a pail of water to heat it for bairns who were helping their mothers with household chores. Harness makers and saddlers sat in lofts, repairing or relining traces and collars for small firms to have them ready for the following morning. When work at the smiddy was slack, a mock set of horse-shoes were made, and tips of the trade passed on to apprentices, who were told that 'horse's hide is nae use for makin' harness'. Show-pieces made here had sixteen stitches to the inch, and resin thread was rolled for extra strength.

Saturday mornings, pillow cases were also carried in order to collect 'brokeners', the second-day bread and biscuits.

HAZLEHEAD PARK

The nineteenth-century house with features by the architect John Smith was replaced by a self-service cafe in 1957. The lodge and steading survive.

In Hazledene Road, there is the nineteenth-century wellhead of the well spring of Nether-town. It is a memorial to William Rose.

HILL STREET
From Rosemount Place to Skene Square

A prehistoric grave was desecrated on this hilltop last century. A clear view of another standing stone at Gallow Hill, the other side of the Loch, could be had.

Hirpletillim, Rubislaw.

DAAVIT DRAIN O' HIRPLETILLIM

There's nae sic men a-makin' noo,
As ane I kent near Rubislaw Quarries,
His een are closed, cauld, cauld his broo,
He's deen wi' a' life's cares and sharries;
Daavit Drain o' Hirpletillim,
Drink never yet was brew'd wad fill him;
Stout an' swack, broad breist, straucht back
Gaed strength and swing to Hirpletillim.

Bauld Daavit wis an auctioneer
At plenishin's he flourish't bravely
His 'going gone' rang firm an' clear
Slow higglers he admonished gravely.

Hirpletillim was Rubislaw's wee village. Its pantiled cottages with old-fashioned gardens have now been replaced by a villa at number 6 Rubislaw Den South,

Old Holburn junction, and Alford Place, named after the Donside village. Bawbie Law's shop was actually up stone steps in Wellington Place. It was said that 'her word was her bond, for she niffer't nae less; shoppie weel stocket, door seldom locket'.

HOLLAND STREET

From Rosemount Place to Skene Square

This street name was suggested by Messrs Richards & Co in 1889 and adopted.

> Servants lookit fine fin they're dressed up tae click
> an' dressmakers look better still;
> but the bonniest lass o' the hale rick-ma-tick
> is the lassie wha works at the mill.

HUNTLY STREET

From Union Street to Rose Street

The pride of Huntly Street is one of Aberdeen's three cathedrals. Its spire reaches a height of two hundred feet.

The rich had to leave their granite mansions behind them, but were sure to be seen off by a crowd of several hundred eager to hear the contents of the will. It was not unusual for twenty Rolls Royce cars to gather for the occasion.

The Asylum and workshop for blind people made the street a household name; but John Smith's impressive building which served their needs since 1843 has been made into office accommodation for an oil company, and renamed Princewall House.

Opposite the Blind Asylum stands Old Free Gilcomston Chapel. It was converted into the Albert Hall and is now warehousing.

The street was named after the Marquis of Huntly in 1820.

HOLBURN STREET

From Union Street to the Brig o' Dee

The new road south over the Howeburn from which it takes its name was a dusty thoroughfare, with glossy country horses often appearing grey before they reached town. Dung carts were driven here daily to riverside gardens from city stables.

Showpiece saddles and hems were made for ploughing matches at the old saddler's shop at Ruthrieston. Nearby was the market stance where Highland Games used to be held. The Howeburn has two sources; one from Hazlehead and another from Craigiebuckler, and there are two courses forming an island at the back of Union Grove. The Ashley burn is a tributary.

Forbes Morrison, slater, of 97 Holburn Street. A small man with a great sense of humour . . . he and Nelson of Trafalgar would have related to each other, both possessing one eye. 'I've only ae' e'e but it' a wheeker!' was one of his favourite sayings.

HOWBURN PLACE

From the Hardgate to Holburn Street

This is the original etymology of Aberdeen's Holburn, which is mistakenly associated with the street in the city of London. The howe is south of the street in question. In the grounds of Bethany House was a draw well which never ran dry.

Huntly Street from the corner of Chapel Street. 👆

HUTCHEON STREET

From Causewayend to 'Killing Hoose' Corner (George Street), and from there past the old station ticket office to Westburn Road

Named after Hugh Hutcheon, an influential advocate in 1806.

To most Aberdonians, the street is associated with 'the Broadford Lum' and 'the Killing Hoose', where 'the killers' dined out on trestles, under the meat-hooks.

Established in 1830 by Mr John Stewart the works occupied premises of almost four acres and was four storeys high. At the turn of the century a rival company was formed at Kittybrewster called the Scottish Comb Company but did not last long, it was taken over by the Combworks. By 1904 1000 people were employed in turning 6,000,000 horns, hoofs and tortoiseshells into 25,000,000 combs a year, of which there were 2000 varieties.

Messrs S. R. Stewart turned out items in diverse materials such as horn, tortoise shell, ivory, wood, metal and composite materials. Their buildings of 1836 were added to in 1880.

The last visible part of the Lochlands survived alongside Hutcheon Street until around the time of the First World War. In 1911, William Daniels, an apprentice of J. & J. Ingram's cartwright shop took a loan of a wee rowing boat along with another apprentice and rowed across the waters of the Loch, and was chased along the bank by a foreman of Broadfords. A few years later he took over the firm, and they were commended upon having steel-ringed 163 gun carriage wheels in one day. During the war Mr Daniels was at Hill 60 on the Somme when he was ordered to fix a broken wheel; it bore his own number 85868.

A horse-drawn delivery van made by J. 👉 & J. Ingram for Leith, the Royal Baker at Ballater. The firm also built barrows and striped carts.

James H. Kissach's Emporium at 136 Hutcheon Street.

INNES STREET
From Gallowgate to Loch Street

This street was opened in 1813, and paved twenty years later. The Innes family of Learney were noted nineteenth-century scholars on the science of name derivation for genealogical research.

Nine people to a room and eight tenants to a lavatory . . . ; there was overcrowding in this street.

JACKSON TERRACE
From Colville Place to Urquhart Lane

There is an inscription on the wall of a house adjoining King Street School. It reads:

Ne'er ye mind
fut fowk say;
bit dee ye weel
an' lat them say.

This is a variant upon Marischal College's official Motto. It is also worth mentioning two versions of another proverb:

I have been to Aberdeen, so can change my mind.

An Aberdeen's man may take his word again.

Justice Lane (middle right)

JAMAICA STREET
From Lamond Place to Calsayseat Road

This street was formed c.1888. The local story has it that there was originally a wooden-house here, and associations with a sea captain who plied on the trades route to West Indies and the southern states of America. Did this story ever reach the ears of Robert Louis Stevenson, author of *Treasure Island*?

JOHN STREET
From Woolmanhill to Loch Street

Rodger's Brig to the Lochlands was first erected in 1801, alongside the Dyer's Well. William Cadenhead's poem concerning the parish of St. George's in-the-West describes the area before the spacious street held sway:

Carters frequented John Street, because near the Woolmanhill, Wordies had a depot. Every morning, fleets of horse lorries left Wordies for the railway station by way of the Denburn Road.

Mr Gladstone's plinth was the pride of Wright's granite yard in John Street; for upon receiving the freedom of the city in 1871, he declared, 'Not a drop of blood runs in my veins except Scotch blood. A large share of my heart has ever belonged to, and will belong to Scotland.'

The North of Scotland Bank was erected on the George Street Corner in 1873, to cater for 'the steadily increasing business of the cattle trade'.

JUSTICE LANE
From Justice Street to East North Street

The line of this street follows the north-west boundary wall of the Castlegate market stance. It used to emerge under an arch into East North Street beside Mither Mac-Donald's Bar.' 'Billy Bruce used to stand his fruit cart in the lane,' writes Jock Mearns. 'The house on the right hand side of the lane facing The Salvation Army Citadel was where Lebbie Annan bided; her lum was always

smoking on washing day'. Mr Robertson's bantam chased away strangers. Madam Rutherford stayed in the house on the far left nearest 'The Port'. She told fortunes for 'The Theatre People' who arrived in gigs dressed to high heavens.'

Upper Justice Mill Brae (or Odeon Brae as it was often called) had at the foot of it an old smiddy run by Johnny Munro who, due to lack of his trade, repaired bicycles. As a joke, he often approached a prospective customer with a five-pound mash hammer in his hand saying, 'Yer three speeds nae warkin afa' weel, I'll jist give it a wee bit tap'.

JUSTICE MILLS
From Union Glen to Justice Mill Lane

The Howeburn provided motivation for the water wheels of both Upper and Lower Justice Mills. Old Mill Road led to the Mill-toun which was surrounded by croftlands. Maids no longer 'rinse their claes in the cauld mill lade,' which since 1931 has run underground.

Justice Mill Lane.

Poole's Regent Cinema was the first cinema that T. Scott Sutherland designed in Aberdeen. Today it is the last to survive. Thoroughly researched (478 plans and detailed drawings), there was a thirty-foot drop in ground level to allow for, and the millpond alongside Justice Mill had to be drained. Over 5000 people attended the opening show.

KEPPLESTONE

Sir George Reid, President of the Royal Scottish Academy, built St. Lukes and it's high-roofed painting room where he, his brother Samuel the book illustrator, and the other brother Archibald, fellow portrait artist worked. It was said of the latter's portrait of John Colvin, Sacrist of Marischal College that the subject's 'clear black eyes and shrewd but kindly grip about the mouth' were characteristically reproduced. Sir George's portrait of Provost Anderson at the new Trades Hall shows him to be more genial than the official photographs allow for.

KIDD LANE
From Chapel Street to Summer Street

This street is named after Dr Kidd who died in 1834. He was honoured and respected above any man in town whilst he was at the Denburn Parish Church. He may have been appointed to the Chair of Oriental Languages at Marischal College, but when he performed the laying on of hands during communion he simply said, 'Be all good.'

KINCORTH, 'THE SATELLITE CITY'

Great attention was paid to the contours of the ground, 'traffic arteries', and maintaining uninterrupted views over the city, by the winners of the 1937 architectural competition, Messrs Holliday, Gardner-Medwin, and Dennis Winston. Its like was unequalled in Scotland as regards 'elevational value and layout of the varying housing types'. 'No fence cottages' were seen here for the first time in Aberdeen.

☛ Salmon fishers at Foords o' Dee

KING STREET
Originally from Castle Street to Love Lane (St. Peter Street)

King Street begins with stately symmetrical buildings, as if to rival Union Street, but dwindling bye and bye to houses of small dimensions and plain design—'granite rabbit hutches', as Baron Corvo described their prototype. It is a wide enough thoroughfare for the Fire Brigade horses to get up enough speed for the children that followed to see sparks flying from their hooves.

The fire station (1899) itself looks like a Renaissance palace, and with the North Kirk of 1831 is still worthy of its royal name. (The king in question was George III.)

The hotel proprietor who made the name of the Royal Atheneum was chosen by Jimmy Hay. He was John Mitchell, who, with his wife ran the County Hotel in King Street. The country buses stopped here to collect passengers, who wisely fortified themselves before braving the 'caul' gabs o' May' on the Newburgh road. Jean Baxter wrote that on 'gaun' hame fae the toon' that the wind outside was as cutting as a knife, but inside, 'the burlin' bus is cosy; in beddit stra' the fermer's wife aneth her bonnet's dosy.'

King Street was famous for its family businesses. Before the bank building was erected, there was a matching block to the one opposite which was originally John E. Esslemont's 'family grocers and Italian warehouse'. They were pioneers in the tea trade, and one of the first in the country to receive Ceylon tea. To attract the public, apprentices dressed in pigtails and packed the tea in a well-dressed window display. 'Tired? We'll refresh you "good as gold",' was their slogan. Alec Booth, master sweep who with his ☛ sons were members of the fire brigade received sixpence per chimney and made his own brushes by dipping the bristles in tar.

On Tuesday 11th April 1911, the largest consignment of sweets ever to come so far north, meant that this was the opportunity to advertise. Esslemont's hired a piper for the occasion, and Mr John Minty led the procession, with an impressive show of the workforce of the shore posters. Twenty-two horse lorries were used.

The Militia Barracks were capable of housing some eight hundred men from the Royal Regiment of Aberdeen Highlanders. W. S. Gilbert, the dramatist of the Gilbert & Sullivan operas, served in the regiment, and no doubt in those days appeared as a 'gallant braw John Heelanman,' with 'his philabeg an' Tartan plaid, an' guid claymore doon by his side'.

The motto of the Fire Brigade is 'Ready, aye ready'.

The opening of King Street caused the removal of one of the public dung stances in 1802. Even into the 1820s King Street was wild and desolate-looking. The New Inn occupied the place where the bank now stands, but did not extend so far eastwards as it does. The large house next to it had been cut through in the formation of King Street, which had on its west side a high rubble bank, on the top of which stood a number of rickety tenements, the occupiers of which had a very bad character. The entrance to this 'rookery' was through a court. Next to these houses was the entrance to the Poultry Market between two brick walls. This spot was the pitch of the matchsellers. There were no buildings on the side of St. Andrew's Cathedral which was occupied by MacDonald's Stoneyard. Stone polishing recommenced in 1772, but it seemed that the manners of Mr MacDonald's partner, Provost Leslie were roughened and also in need of polishing. Nevertheless they obligingly departed to Constitution Street so that the Metropolitan Improvements could proceed.

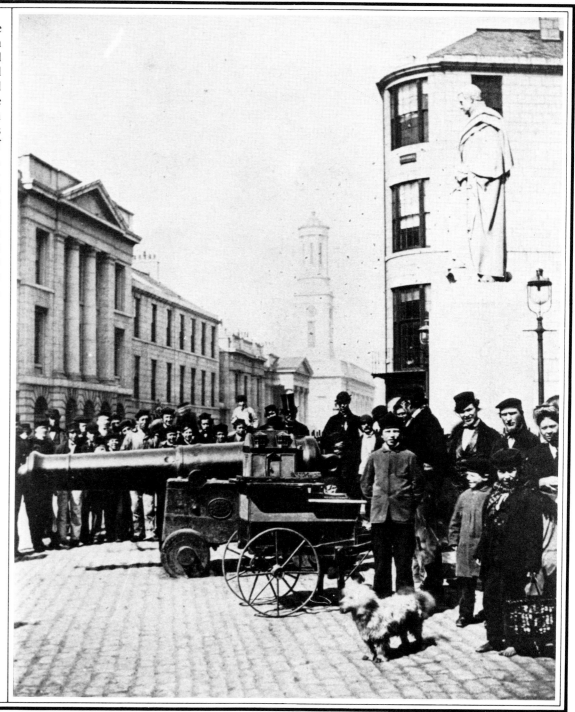

Harold Cooper (third left) was owner of The King's Bar, 97 King Street.

The Granite Duke and Balaclava Cannon; a stereoscopic view of Castle Street and King Street corner, taken by George Washington Wilson. Shore porters and street porters as well as a hurdy gurdy man are amongst the crowd of 'East Neuk Worthies'. In 1830, fishwives selling dulse formed a row extending in the line of King Street. Behind them was a row of carts filled with north country crabs and fishes. A group of milk girls who, as soon as anyone was seen approaching with a vessel of any kind, would pester purchasers, and give them a tonguing if after all they decided not to buy anything at all.

KINGSLAND PLACE

From the Barkmill burn to Hutcheon Street

The street can now be found between 343/347 George Street. It has a namesake in London, the Kingsland Road.

LANGSTANE PLACE

From Crown Street to Bon-Accord Terrace

Originally referred to as the head of Dee Street, where the Langstane is actually situated.

The landmark of the Langstane Kirk, with its beadle's house and cathedral glass was opened in 1869.

Leadside Road had some of the city's earliest tenements. They can be seen behind Police Box number 19.

Ma Cameron's farin' for men an' Horses. Timmer Market wares are sold at the door, whilst business is transacted with the carrier inside.

LEADSIDE ROAD

From Esslemont Avenue (originally from Short Loanings) to Stevenson Street and South Mount Street (originally known as 'Gilcomston Brae')

On leaving the Dam of Gilcomston, the head of which was at Prince Arthur Street and Osborne Place, the Denburn split into two, and the old lade which gave its name to the locality ran along, quite open on the right-hand side of what was a country road; with little bridges here and there giving right of way to those who had property on the south side. The road has been altered by the laying out of new streets, and the building of the Grammar School. The first bridge led over to the Model Gardens, a series of 'plotties', partially on the site of the playground. Immediately past this, another bridge led to Chadwick's woollen mill, the wheel of which was driven by water from the lade. The mill was burned down sometime in the fifties or sixties, and was not set working again. Close to the open lade near the foot of Short Loanings there were dwelling houses reached by a bridge from the north side. At the top of Jack's Brae the lade was covered, so that cart traffic could have access to the Northfield weaving sheds.

LIME STREET

From Waterloo Quay to St. Clement Street

The Lime Basin was filled in during 1835. The quay stretching from Commerce Street was known as the 'Lime Quay'. Boats were punted over from the Lime Sheds where they were loaded into the Canal Basin, then hauled to their destination by horses along the bank.

The present street is c.1853.

LITTLE BELMONT STREET

From Back Wynd to Belmont Street

Where purchases were deposited for out-of-town delivery for the carrier. There was a smell of singed hoof and tar at the smiddy, where the apprentices' first lesson was to 'cha' bogie roll'. Boys who attended the town's new schools here thought that Aberdeen was the capital of Scotland.

Ma Cameron's Inn is one of the few bars to survive from the coaching age. Even though its peat fires are a thing of the past in it's 'snug', until recently the stables in the old cobbled courtyard survived with the faded names of horses on timber posts. The street was paved in 1831.

LITTLEJOHN STREET

From Gallowgate to West North Street

The street was approached through an archway from Gallowgate and was named after William Littlejohn when it was completed in 1764. The firm of John Blaikie and Sons carried on the business of braziers, bell and brass founders, plumbers, gasfitters and coppersmiths from their two-storey metal works, some of which have been incorporated into the grounds of Marischal College.

LOCH HEAD

A mansion complete with Turkish and medicated baths, it was the first 'Hydro' in Scotland. It was situated in Westburn Road and was demolished in 1932 after it had housed the George Washington Wilson & Co magic lantern slide export department. These slides were buried under concrete adjacent to the site of the mansion.

LOCHLANDS

The Lochlands covered an elongated area of more than a hundred acres, starting at the north end at Fraser Road to Millbank Lane; then to Holland Street where the Westburn entered. The deepest part was south of Hutcheon Street, banked by Kingsland Place, Maberly Street, Spring Garden, Loch Street, Crooked Lane, St. Andrews Street and Blackfriars Street. The outlet was at Gilcolmston Steps, and the high bank was at Ann Street. It was fordable at the north end, and at the making of the gate of Broadford Works, 18 feet of peat containing hazel stems were dug up showing the extent of the Lochlands.

Lochlands Bairnies

Bonnie Loch
O' Aiberdeen,
Biggit ower
Wi' Granite stane!

Biggit ower
But an' ben,
Fae Kingsland Place
T' Crooked Lane!

Biggit ower
For gweed or ill,
Fae Gallow Gate
T' Woolman Hill.

Biggit ower
In a' but name.
Happit up
Wi' hoose and hame.

Weesht! Hark!
Bairnies' feet
Treetlin ben
John Street.

Wha's bairnies
Micht they be?
Lochland bairnies!
Come and see,

Elfin faces,
Twinklin een
Like the starnies
O' yestreen,

In the bonnie
loch that lay
Ayont Black Freers
Mony a day,

When Wee Folks danced
Their Magic Spell
Upon the Play Green,
Near the Well,

Or speelin up
The Woolman Hill
Wi' fite Maw's feeder
And grey goose quill,

A different kind of 'Wallie Dog'.

Gaed hipperty hopperty
Doon the Steps
In sarkets green
And velvet keps,

To cweel their taes
In the water clear,
Fleggin the wits
O' John the Freer

Warslin doon
Fae Black Freers Manse
To catch a trootie
By grace or chance:

Syne hipperty Skipperty
Up Scoole Hill
For a Pixy Jig
In the Grammar Skweel,

Or to play tick-an'-tack
Roon the kirkyard stanes
Wi' Ghaist Raw ghosties
In their teens,

Till Auld St. Nicholas
Cou'dna sleep
Though he coontit hunners
O' black-faced sheep:

And past the vennel
And Wyndmill Hill,
Through Gallow Gate Port
Wi' right gweed will,

Roon Leper's Croft
Like a flaucht O' fire,
To Cunninghar Holes
and Futtiesmyre,

And lipperty lapperty
Ower the links,
To Futty Kirk
In Forty Rig,

Or clickerty Clackerty
Ower Thieves Brig,
By Bowack Croft
and Penny Rig,

Through Justice Port
Or Futties Wynd,
The Castlehill
Was Left behind,

And Mercat Cross
And Castlegate-
Crickity crick,
'Twas gettin late.

Picherty Pecherty
Up the Hill,
Past the Chapel
And Friar Will

As he coontit his beads
Wi' a side-long glance,
Or lay a-snorin
In Trinity Manse,

To Carmelite Place
And alang the Green
Whaur Bruce and the Lion
Rode yestreen,

Across Bow Brig,
Up Windmill Brae,
To the Lang stan'in
This mony a day,

and helterty skelterty
Ower the rig
O'Corby Heugh
In a whirligig,

And hip hooray.
Ower Burn and Denn.
Hark. A horn.
Puff. They're gane.

March Lane looking towards Jack's
Brae.

LOCH STREET

From Crooked Lane and Harriet Street to Spring Garden

Loch Street follows the bank of the Loch. In 1888 there was a scheme to extend it to Hutcheon Street and Causewayend. Even in 1632 the Loch was described as being 'filthillie defyllit and corruptit; not only by gutteris daylie rynning in the burne, but also litstaris and the washing of clothes and abusing of the water in sundrie partis with other sortis of uncleannes.'

Smiling ladies, who in exchange for a ticket gave those in need 'soup in a bowlie, a slice o' breid and meatbane stew; with a cup o' tea, what mair wid ye expect for free', at the Soup Kitchen.

In a shop opposite, 'Candy Bell' sold owls' eye eggs, cupid whispers and conversation lozenges. Pink peardrops gleamed like jewels in glass jars, and near a tray of treacle dabs, a white parrot kept watch, biting the children who dared to touch it.

The street became a household name, not only for the factory of 'Soapy' Ogston, but for the co-op Arcade. 'The Coopie' had eight motor delivery vans before the First World War, but children were even quicker at running the odd message to either 'the butter side' or 'the sugar side', and any Aberdonian worth his salt remembers his mother's 'Coopie number'.

☛ The Arcade could also be entered from the Gallowgate. It was very handy, as you could get everything under the one roof. In those days, a voucher was issued for purchases which could include bakery sundries, groceries, butcher meat, shoes, clothes, bedding, furniture, fancy goods, china, toys and games.

Fire at Ogston and Tennant's Soap Works
Saturday, 13th August, 1904

The Fire at Ogston & Tennant 13th August 1904.

LODGE WALK

From Castle Street to Queen Street

The original street which ran at right angles to the present foreshortened street, which is dominated by The Grampian Police Headquarters. It dates back to 1754 when The Aberdeen Lodge moved into upstairs chambers at The New Inn, leaving their isolated meeting room at Futtie's Myre Croft. When The New Inn was sold in 1839 and the bank premises built, the re-alignment took place. This was made possible by the removal of 'the horseshoe staircase' outside the Tolbooth in 1818. There was room for small traders to have a stance in this street.

Bairns chanted this street song about one of these traders; it is dated c.1790:

Willie o' The Wall,
an' Sawney o' The Meen,
wha gae'd up Castle Street
an' ran doon the Green.
That's Willie o' The Wall
in his verra little stall;
sits Willie o' The Wall.

The wall referred to is the one used to photograph the bobbies against:

Fa' wid like tae be a bobby,
Dressed up in funny clothes;
Wi' a belly fu' o' fat
An' a great big tarry hat,
An' a big mealy pudden for a nose?

Big feet, bap feet—
hear the bairnies cry
every ilkie morning
when they're plodding by—
They're chappin' at yer windies,
and crying through yer lock,
are a' youse bairnies in bed
it's past eight o'clock.

The gaol of Aberdeen was at one time the Tolbooth; subsequently the East Prison which stood nearby was built.

But noo Hope is in the past,
for forgery I've been ta'en,
and here I lie to wait my trial
in The Gaol O' Aberdeen.
(An extract from the ballad 'Jock Scott')

The Burgh Courthouse of Queen Anne's time had fluted pillars and acanthus leaf capitals. Some of these were saved and incorporated into a summer house at Duthie Park along with some old carvings from St. Nicholas Kirk.

LONG ACRE
From Broad Street to West North Street

A passageway which was one of the city centre short cuts, leading also to Henderson's and Jopp's Courts. Wesley preached here, but his chapel 1795 later became a warehouse.

The street was laid out in 1784, and is named after the London thoroughfare which although it is wider, may be said not to have concentrated such a range of skills behind its frontages. The Aberdeen Long Acre comprised a pawnbroker, a spirit dealer, two dressmakers, a funeral waiter, milliner, shoemaker, surgeon, midwife, teacher, horse shoer, grocer, plasterer, printer and cooper, and radical newspapers known as *Aberdeen Pirate*, and *Aberdeen Shaver*. Mr Grant the teacher, was successor to the famous 'Budsie' Bowers who taught Byron at the Long Acre Academy. He was reputed to have kicked his pupils and applied the tawse somewhat liberally.

MABERLY STREET
Originally from Broadford Gate to Skene Square

The street perpetuates the memory of John Maberly, proprietor of the works at Broadford, and Rubislaw Bleachfields. He was also a banking pioneer. He died in France, a broken man, in 1845. His brother, on the other hand, invented a mechanical street scavenger, and lived a more fulfilled life.

Power loom weaving was established in Aberdeen By Mr Maberly in 1824. By 1864 six steam engines turned 428 looms and 16,814 spindles for flax and tow. 2175 people were employed. They moved to the north bank of the Dee in 1904 on the site of the old bleachfields.

It was an old saying amongst working men who intended getting married that it was a case of

Spring Garden for Poverty,
The Wool Mill for pride—
The Boag Mill for a bonnie lass;
and Broadford for a bride.

In the secluded walled gardens of Broadford Cottage, members of Aberdeen's intelligentsia gathered for musical evenings. Culture flew out of the window as the place was torn down in the early 1890s.

Then let us hail the factory din
Again wi' cheery smile,
An' bless the bell wha's welcome soond
Invites us tae oor toil:
Lang may we timely thrang the gates,
Wi' grateful hert an' will,
At gathering an' at lowsin' hour—
O' guid auld Broadford Mill.
W. Cadenhead (1898)

MACKIE PLACE
Off Skene Street

At number six Mackie Place there was a haunted house known as the 'Castle' or the 'Galleries'. An intellectual group of people, who wrote poetry and journal articles, met there. They published "the Castle Spectre". Dressed in white sheets, they jumped out on passers by. Grotesque faces were carved out of turnips, the candles lit, and stuck in hedges around Cherryvale to frighten away inquisitive bairns. The town watchman did not go further than the foot of Jack's Brae. One of the carefree residents, Miss Forbes, wrote a few lines about the Denburn:

Beneath two giant willows that stand before our door, the Denburn runs so sweetly with its green and silvery shore.

But sometimes it is flooded and then the torrent's roar is like the sound near Buffaloe where hearing is no more; when down comes sticks and turnips, and tumbles down the wall.

Oh! what a hurry scurry when you think the bridge will fall.

This was published in 'The Castle Spectre'.

The street was named after Robert Mackie, a skinner who was Convener of the Incorporated Trades. Two fine Georgian houses with ogee gables still survived from his day.

MAGDALA PLACE
Off Short Loanings

This street was named by an Aberdonian who had witnessed the Storming of Magdala, in Ethiopia.

Da says ye micht hae sair han's at Broadfords,
but its better than hain' weet caul feet at the fish.

THE DINNER HOUR AT BROADFORD WORKS, ABERDEEN.

Mackie Place Bridge.

MARCH LANE

From Jack's Brae to the 'backies' in Esslemont Avenue

This is one of the Aberdeen byeways that has vanished from the street plan of the city, yet unbelievably it is still in existence, even if in somewhat of a tattered state complete with the Communal Royalty Stones that were inspected when the boundaries were checked on the ceremony of the Riding of The Inner Marches. There were bleachfields here and the Denburn ran in 'troughs.'

MARINE TERRACE

From the west side of South Crown Street

Once the home of sea captains, and amongst the short leet of Granite City streets to have had the first gleaming Bentley limousines standing in readiness outside these Ferryhill front doors.

Designed by Archibald Simpson, the terrace had a fine 'view' over Aberdeen harbour. Now it is stranded on a yellow bank of daffodils, dreaming of sailing ships; while down the hill at Prospect Terrace, there is no longer the prospect that there used to be. Young lovers

No. 6 Mackie Place as viewed from The Grammar School Grounds before Esslemont Avenue was erected. The photograph is after 1870, the date when the memorial church to Samuel Rutherford was opened in Rosemount Place. Its spire can be seen rising above the houses in Short Loanings.

admired the expanse of wild flowers that bloomed, out of reach, over on the Inches (islets in the River Dee that survived until the 1880s, when a vast land reclamation plan was carried out; even a scheme to deflect the Dee artificially to the Bay of Nigg was seriously considered). The original banks of the River Dee are indicated by Bank Street.

To Marischal Street we steppit ower,
the only road then to the Shore,
saw shore porters at heavy tasks
up the street haulin' great big casks
on a laigh buggy wi' four wheels
took a' their strength, though gey stout chiels;
carryin' great loads the Shore up frae,
by Marischal Street and Hangman's Brae,
tired ere to the heid they got it,
were stout men, and widnae knottit.

James Smith (1830)

When these houses in Mackie Place 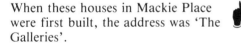 were first built, the address was 'The Galleries'.

MARISCHAL STREET

From Castle Street to Regent Quay

Before 1765, there was no direct public access from Castle Street to the Quay. Consequently the gabled town residence of the Earls Marischal was taken down, and a new street paved with squared granite setts was constructed on arches, which made convenient stables for the new houses. Artists such as the pre-Raphaelite, William Dyce, and Andrew Robertson, a miniature artist, were born here, and at number 46, William Kennedy the advocate wrote *The Annals of Aberdeen* (1818).

Shakespeare is said to have visited Aberdeen in October 1601. The local witch trials gave him background material for *Macbeth*. A bar in Marischal Street was named after him. The chief loss to Marischal Street has been Scotland's first flyover, Bannerman's Bridge, although the firm of George Thompson & Co at 60 Marischal Street that ran the Aberdeen line of steamers and sailing ships became better known. Cattle too were sent deck passage to London.

Come and see my garret
come up and see it noo—
come up and see my garret
'cause it's a' mistrew.
A humpty backit dresser,
a chair wi'oot a leg,
a three legged table and
an auld iron bed.   Anon.

MARKET STREET

From Union Street to Victoria Bridge

Market Street was laid out 1840–2 and is constructed on arches over the site of an impoverished part of the town known as Putachieside.

Through the steam from the harbour engine's funnel, polo-necked seamen with their black bags over their shoulders headed for the ships. Tracer horses, having hauled loads of steel up the hill, stopped and rested at St. Nicholas Street whilst their chains were removed. Boys placed wedge-shaped blocks of wood under the carriages and held their jackets over the wheels so that those alighting wouldn't be in the dubs. Hence the expression 'scotched'.

Harness sometimes would not take the gradient, but all went well on 2nd July 1881 when a procession of the Town Council went in carriages to open the £25,000 Victoria Bridge. The 345-foot long structure was the pride of John Fyfe, granite merchant of Kemnay. The bridge presents the strange appearance of having two archways through each pier. This is because masonry was built upon the top of the caissons, and the three small piers joined together above water by two arches.

Much could also be learnt about the city, besides turning the musty pages of leather-bound books that made it seem that the Bodleian Library of Low's bookstall had burst up there in the massive roof.

Children were always to be seen looking into 'the penny-in-the-slot' machine at the Union Street lobby, where a fireman gallantly rescued a woman from a burning room. The New Market was itself burnt down despite the efforts of the old handpumps of the fire brigade. When it was reopened, the share-holders voted that the stalls could be let free for a week.

The refined forcefulness of Archibald Simpson's New Market design (1840–2), 'was adapted from the basilicas of Rome'.

When it opened on 29 April 1842, choirs and pipebands were in attendance.

You could buy almost anything in this universal store; it was known for its distinct blend of smells. Merchants in the gallery provided a range of trinkets and services. Ears could be pierced, bodies tattooed, watches engraved and fortunes told.

Market Street had some other important public buildings, namely the Mechanic's Institute, the Bon Accord Hotel and the General Post Office on the east side of the street at numbers seven and nine. Market Street Post Office was built in 1875 on the site of the retail fish market.

☛ 46 & 48 Marischal Street.

MARTIN'S LANE

From the Green to Rennie's Wynd

This street had a smiddy adjoining Rennie's Wynd, and it was handy for re-shoeing, if any emergencies happened to town horses in the vicinity of the Station yard. Washing hung out of the windows from long poles, and the men-folk who stood at their doors in the evening smoking 'cheekwarmer' pipes wore their bonnets 'aft agley', and a pair of moleskin trousers was likewise worn with panache.

MARYWELL STREET

From South College Street to Crown Street

A public draw well here, dedicated to St. Mary, was just one of the famous springs of Aberdeen.

It was a century ago that John Ellis, who resided at number eighteen, set up in business as 'a coal merchant and commission agent'. The industrial estates soon to be laid out on the reclaimed bed of the River Dee, nearby, were a thing of the future. Bain's horsebus took folk to work.

MASTRICK

This is now the name of a housing scheme, but was originally a dairy farm with extensive steadings. Provost Ross of Arnage had merchant trading interests in Maastricht, Holland, hence the names Arnage Drive and Mastrick.

MEALMARKET STREET

From King Street to West North Street

This is an old-fashioned street for there are records of its improvement in 1805. Edward Raban, the famous printer 1622–50 had his printing shop above the 'Meil Mercat' on the north side of the Castlegate. The Mealmarket itself was built in 1760, by John Jeans, the architect of the Bow Briggie. At one time there were two breweries here, and the comb-makers Messrs Stewart commenced business in the street as the carrier was handy to uplift orders.

Mealmarket lane . . . that wis
the name that 'twas kent by then;
that name it deserve it weel:
a market for sellin' meal:
In a large square, just off the street,
in covered sheds to keep aff the weet
wi' open fronts, their stores to show,
in front a counter, weights below,
a beam and scales upon the top,
wis halely used as a meal shop

James Smith (1830)

He continues:

A place it's now of steam and fire,
and things that they do mak' oot o' wire;
where once was heard the mealwives'
   clamour,
now is heard the blacksmith's hammer,
anvil's din, and bellows blawin'.

MIDDLETHIRD

From Waterloo Quay to St Clement Street

This street was in existence in 1805.

MILE END

This street name is derived from London's Mile End Road. Aberdeen Council, knowing that London's East End merchants made their money there, decided to let those who had made their way in life have an opportunity of taking their street name with them to the West End. It was originally known as Mile End Heights, and a viewing tower was suggested. The country estates of Raeden, Woodhill, Foresterhill, Rosehill, Cornhill, Ashgrove, Bonnymuir, Burnside and Westburn House could be clearly seen when the trees were bare.

MILLBURN STREET

From South Crown Street to Wellington Road

This street is dominated by the Aberdeen Corporation Electrical Works. The city's coat of arms in granite set in the massive Dutch gable must surely be one of the seven wonders of the Granite City.

MILLER STREET

From Cotton Street to Garvock Street

This street was formerly known as Summer Lane. It was re-named after John Miller of Sandilands Chemical Works, who took a lease on the refuse products of the Gas Works, and manufactured paraffin oil and by-products from coal tar.

Miller Street from Castle Terrace.

MORNINGFIELD

This is a commanding site which was originally occupied by a cluster of cottages of that name. Morningfield Hospital originally occupied grounds at Belleville in the Upper Denburn. This house was purchased with a view to opening up Rosemount as a residential district by means of 'a viaduct'. Now the Hospital for Incurables has ceased to exist, and the fine building that is Morningfield cost £7,000 in 1883.

MOUNTHOOLY

From Gallowgate to Canalside

This was the old route that the street took, but it now lies buried beneath an artificial Mount Hooly. It was anciently spelt Mount Heillie. The real Mount Hooly is surmounted by Ninian Comper's Convent chapel.

MOUNT STREET

From Rosemount Place to Rosemount Terrace

This street was one of the earliest Rosemount streets. It was laid out in 1853, and a reformatory for girls was in operation by 1862.

NORTH STREET, EAST & WEST

By the close of the eighteenth century, this street, now part of the Inner City Link Road, was in existence at the foot of the Gallowhill. Its days of fever-infected backies and overcrowding are over. Its most famous building, the Lodging House, has been home for many of the East End Worthies.

NELSON STREET

From King Street to West North Street

Laid out at the time of the battle of Trafalgar. The only 'charges' that were ever made were by cattle being taken this route to the mart from the Links. Women ran for the safety of shop doors when they heard the pounding of hooves. Mrs Scullion at the corner fish shop sold hot ranns, ovened herring, boiled skate, potted heid and tripe to cinemagoers who wished to 'develop their brains' on the way to the Globe cinema.

McDonald's bakery sold Dargai Buns which were named after the Battle of Dargai Heights in India, Scott Skinner also composed a commemorative fiddle tune.

A phonetic order received at a Haberdashery. (Spelling was not the lady's strong point!)

Sand me 1 pas flann God to sale at 1 a pas
blu prent begg fit spote 30
Yalo dulis 4 haf spinl blackk
wurstit haf grogra with the
Millerts cart a Macfirsns stabls
Waste North Strete.

The astute salesman deciphered it as follows:

1 piece of flannel good to sell at a 1s
1 piece blue print big white spot
30 yds yellow dowlas sell at 4d
½ spindle grow grey worsted
by the Millers cart at Mcphersons
send by stables West North Street

OSBORNE PLACE

From Albert Street to Blenheim Place

Formerly North Carden Place, lined with Golden Elms, and was laid out in 1868. The name Osborne was chosen in 1871 because Queen Victoria had a residence named Osborne in the south of England on the Isle of Wight.

Stonyton Bridge, which crossed over The Denburn at Prince Arthur Street, was a rickety-rackety brig, and it was taken down in 1903. A meal mill at one time got power from the Denburn, and it was situated between Osborne Place and Carden Place. A tributary stream flowed on the south side of Desswood Place, and entered the main burn over Gilcomston Dam, which has now been drained and built over.

PALMERSTON PLACE

From South College Street to North Esplanade West

At this point, the Howeburn runs into the Dee. The street was named after the famous prime minister.

PORK LANE
From Regent Quay to Virginia Street

Coopers, seamen, carters and tailors worked out of this street; their work was concentrated upon the harbour area.

Pork Lane had its own street well, and various cottages were described as being 'salubrious,' however it was found that the soil was saturated with poisonous excretions, so no more houses could be erected upon it. 'Great warehouses for the storage of merchandise' replaced Pork Lane completely.

PORTLAND STREET
From Crown Street to South College Street

Named after a Prime Minister, not the stone quarry in Dorset; Portland Street to most Aberdonians meant Clayhills, and red bricks. An Aberdeen Provost lived here in a house with porch supported with pillars; he was the owner of Clayhills until the lands fell into the hands of an advocate.

The south side of Affleck Street overlooked the claypits. The brick kilns were curiously constructed with massive buttresses, but these were torn down in the 1860s when the market for granite was more brisk. The twenty-two acres of Clayhills saw massive changes. Some of the workshops were then leased to other business concerns: a coal merchant, granite yard, wood merchant, plasterer and stabler flourished there.

Wordies had their depot, Cartwright and Smith's shop at Clayhills, besides being at 'Roger's Walk', John Street, Schoolhill and Bannermill. The company had 335 horses insured for £175 17s. 6d. in the 1870s and did business with Aberdour, Banff, Macduff, Cullen, Cruden Bay, Fraserburgh, Huntly, Inverurie, Lossiemouth, Portsoy, Stonehaven and Turriff. They were linked administratively with Stirling.

In 1830, James Smith visited the market sheds which at that time had tiled roofs. A character that 'abody kent' was 'Turkey Willie'.

'Turkey Willie'.

POULTRYMARKET LANE
Off Queen Street

The Artillery Volunteers had had their Drill Hall in the Old Poultry Market, as did the Engineer Volunteers.

Now, a bit farer up Queen Street
o' seein' sights I got a treat,
on explorin', now embarkit
in to see The Poultry Market;
saw for sale, butter eggs an' cheese,
sellers there (buyers ill to please)
sittin' wi' baskets in their lap.

POWIS
From Powis Place (Causewayend to Powis Terrace

Powis Terrace (George Street to Great Northern Road and Clifton Road) and Powis Avenue, Crescent and Circle take their name from a pool into which ran the Powburn. The latter streets are centred around historic Powis House, and date from 1937.

The Cot Toun of Kittybrewster was obliterated by the railway yard. Train loads of farmers arrived at the passenger station for the bull and gimmer sales. Weatherbeaten shepherds wearing 'plaidies' were sometimes seen in the company.

A Hilton pensioner opened the Astoria Cinema in 1934. Novelties introduced by architect T. Scott Sutherland included an illuminated Compton organ (the first in Scotland), and 'realistic sound reproduction'. There was seating accommodation for 2000, and waiting rooms could hold 500.

South Crown Street looking towards Portland Street, 1903. Aerial photographs were taken from the top of the chimney stack.

Aberdeen Corporation Electricity Works Chimney being constructed, (1901).

Chivas Cairtloons outside the post office in Crown Street.

Looking towards Powis Terrace from the Central Park and Astoria Cinema. In the foreground, the horse trough, (now in Duthie Park), and middle right, Madame Veitch's trailer, where she read fortunes.

POYNERNOOK ROAD

From Market Street to Palmerston Road

Laid out on land once known as the Poyner's Neuk, owned by 'the Pynours' (shore porters).

Tin sheds lined the road, and wooden barrels lined the pavement. Horses delivered the fish and worked from crack of dawn for their masters.

The dung carts went around the city streets very early in the morning. Cinders were also mixed in. There was a public dung stance at Poynernook as early as 1799.

PRINCE REGENT STREET

From Canal Terrace to Miller Street

This street dates from c.1820, when curb stones were laid. Its chief landmark was Old St. Clement's Free Kirk built in 1843, but like everything else in the surrounding streets it is part of 'Aberdeen Awa''.

PRINCES STREET

From King Street to Park Street

The curbs in this street were laid in 1818. As early as 1807, one city lover had his criticisms to voice about the place: 'It is unhappily named; unless it be in compliment to the Prince of Darkness.'

Ross's scrapyard in Princes Street. The ferrous metal is being separated from the non-ferrous.

PUTACHIESIDE

Off Carnegie's Brae and East Green

The upper part of Market Street is supported by a long arch spanning Putachieside. Putachie means: a place where there was a cattlefold beside a burn. In early Aberdeen Burgh Records there was grazing ground on either side of the Denburn for the cows of the burghers. Now . . .

The Mautmill Burn's a' cover'd up;
Its course ye wadna ken—
An' a'thing's turned heels-o'er-heads
Aboot oor aul' gate-en'

High-minded the west end of Aberdeen may be, but nurse-maids fondly referred to landmarks. They were sure to point out the 'Tartan Kirkie' to their young charges. The kirk is remarkable for the use made of variagated granite in the style of William Butterfield.

There was flooding from the millburn as late as 1837, and the street which was described as being 'one of the meanest and filthiest streets in the city; a confused rookery of some ruinous buildings and tortuous dark and dirty alleys thronged with ill-clad crowds and hosts of squalling children. A. Brown & Co the famous Aberdeen bookseller had a shop here, along with a cabinet maker, hostler, saddler and coachman.

One of the better-known residents was 'Methodist Meg' but everybody had moved out by 1841. The squared setts in the main street and a courtyard survived as the floor of the vaults, where for a time the famous Putachieside whisky was kept in bond.

🖑 QUEEN'S CROSS

At the junction of Albyn Place, Carden Place, St. Swithin Street, Fountainhall Road, Queen's Road, and Queen's Gardens

When the statue of Queen Victoria by C. B. Law (1893) was placed in a regal position, looking towards Balmoral, yet within view of a certain resident's front door, by Messrs Ross's crane, in 1964, a councillor received a complaint about an 'East End Personage' being moved to the West End . . . otherwise known as 'The Queen'.

George Washington Wilson, who was asked to take photographic likenesses of the Royal family, lived at number one Queen's Cross, in a villa shaped like a clover leaf. Russell Mackenzie the architect provided him with a set of weathervanes that had to be greased regularly, and a central heating system. The yellow pine moulds for the cornices and ceiling roses were specially made. Peacocks, thistles and fruit adorned the walls above the brass picture rails. Wallpaper was hand printed, and imported from Italy in tin containers. Woodwork received five coats, and everything was sealed until the painters had finished applying the egg shell enamel.

On his photographic assignments, George Washington Wilson shoed his own horse, ate dried venison and 'brazie mutton' (savoury sausages made from sheep found dead in the hills). When he slept out in mountainside bothies his straw bed was sprinkled with cheap and powerful whisky to kill the bugs.

50 Queens Road.

QUEEN'S ROAD

From Queen's Cross to the former city boundary

The inscription that John Morgan designed for his bookplates reads 'The house the lord builds not—we vainly strive to build it'. His gothic home at 50 Queen's Road (1887) by J. B. Pirie is neverthelesss a family home, as are all the villas with attic billiard rooms and panelled studies. The Grammar School Former Pupils' Club building at Bayview is also worthy of mention. The south side of Queen's road up to Bayview owes it's uniformly good proportions because a syndicate had a say in the building of it. The architect in charge was A. M. Mackenzie. Aberdeenshire Cricket Club occupied the site of the Convent of the Sacred Heart. This range of buildings were the inspiration of Robert Fletcher, but because it lay empty for years it was known as 'Fletcher's Folly'.

QUEEN STREET

From Broad Street to West North Street

Named after the Queen of George III; the gracious surroundings and cobbled yards where carriages were drawn in off the street are no more. Here was the old playhouse, and the county showed their approval of the place, for Earl Aberdeen's commissioner had a residence here which later became the office of the *Aberdeen Herald* until it ceased publication in 1876. The building was demolished for the University extensions.

Marcus Milne has described this thoroughfare dating back to 1773 as 'ha'in the maist hame-o'er figures that iver baked a bap, or presided o'er a toon cooncil.' One such personage was 'Statio Ross', a china mender from Lodge Walk nearby. Besides calling at the doors seeking old china to mend he had a peepshow at the Castlegate on Fridays, but he was said to have slandered Colonel Leith and was incarcerated for a month; meanwhile his box, trestle and pictures were burnt by the hangman. . . .

Grey goose quills were made in Shoe Lane nearby, and sent to London by boat. Work started early in the morning, but Queen Street's shops, down steps were also open late. Customers called in by on their way to the Banks of Ythan. They had no intention of going for a country walk—this was a place for drinking men.

RAEBURN PLACE

From Gilcomston Park to Spa Street

This tenement was named after Peter Raeburn, baker, of Schoolhill, and Deacon of the Incorporation of Bakers, and not the great Scottish artist. The use of rose pink granite from the Hill o' Fare makes this an oasis in a sea of grey granite.

ROSE STREET FROM UNION STREET, ABERDEEN.

RAGG'S LANE

From Broad Street at 37 to Guestrow

The name of Baillie Ragg, who died in 1719, was remembered here.

RAIK ROAD

From Palmerston Road to North Esplanade West

Built on reclaimed land from the floodplain of the River Dee, the name is derived from old and well-known salmon fishings on the Dee.

RICHMOND STREET

From Leadside Road to Rosemount Place

A tenement street that has survived nearly intact from the 1870s. Built of coursed rubble, it predates the Golden Age of tenement building, 1880–1910.

ROSE STREET

From Union Street to the Bridewell

The Bridewell, or West Prison lay behind a fourteen-foot high wall with a garden and airing grounds; it was in use from 1809–70. An entrance arch was flanked by a porter's lodge and guardhouse. The prison may not have looked like the Bastille but it was five storeys high. Nearby was the Aberdeen Carriage Works, who made phaetons, landaus, governess' cars, pony carriages and waggonettes. John Clark, the proprietor, liked to paint his wheels in a bright yellow, that when revolving they had the appearance of 'blazing orbs'. Another manufacturer here

 Looking up Rose Street from Union Street towards the site of the Bridewell.

that catered for the Age of Refinement was Messrs Harrott who specialised in ladies' gloves, hosiery and woollens. Few could have matched Provost George Henry, whose linen and high shirt collars were spotless. The Circuit Court Judge thought that he was an agent for the British Linen Company. George Henry, who was Lord Provost 1850–3 and still powdered his hair in the old-fashioned way, was honoured by having a short street that led up to the ladies' prison, named after him.

ROSLIN STREET

From Park Road to Seaforth Road

This tenement street was laid out in 1893, by the Incorporated Trades.

ROSEMOUNT PLACE

From Skene Square to Beechgrove Terrace

Formerly a country road (from Farmers' Hall to Mile End being garden ground, with spacious villas like Belvidere and Wallfield, standing in their own policies).

A tracer horse was required at Stevenson Street to haul the open deck horse tram up the brae to Wallfield. William Bain's horse buses had served the district until 1872.

The Skene Street corner of Rosemount Viaduct.

119

ROSEMOUNT VIADUCT
From Schoolhill to South Mount Street

The New South Free kirk, St. Marks, by Matthews & Mackenzie was the first of the trio 'Education', 'Salvation' and 'Damnation' to be erected in 1890. The Central Library followed in 1892, the theatre last, but not least. The Schoolhill Railway station is now demolished but it formed a quartet, being 'Transportation'.

St. Paul's United Free kirk of 1897 and Messrs Ironside's Duty Free Warehouses, now a shopping parade, are the other outstanding landmarks.

 William Wallace on his pedestal of unhewn granite blocks, the building of the theatre is in progress.

Weel, weel aul' Aiberdeen,
A something there's aboot ye
That grips wir hert an' weets wir een.
We couldna dae withoot ye.

The Theatre Staff.

The Milkboy.

St. Mark's Church showing Blacks Buildings, (right).

ROSEMOUNT SQUARE

Bounded by South Mount Street, Leadside Road, Richmond Street and Kintore Place

Originally this was the Aladdin's Cave of Cocky Hunter's store, but this perished in a fire, and was replaced by the model flats, which appropriately have granite sculptures of the elements placed over arched entrances.

'Rosemount Vienna' dates from 1937, and belongs to the heyday of the collaboration between the City Architect A. B. Gardner and T. Scott Sutherland. The four-storey flats may have attracted criticism, but there can be no argument that 'a Viennese whirl' has emerged from C. & D. Morton's preserves factory site.

Architect T. Scott-Sutherland on his Triumph, 1921.

ROTUNDA PLACE, FERRYHILL

This name is an *aide-mémoire* for 'The Round "O"', or "Whirlabout". In 1611, it is mentioned in a lease for 'The Pilmuir', and referred to 'The Pott callit "The Roundabout" on the Moss of Ferriehill'; and in 1746 as 'The Hill formation described as a considerable space—a circular quagmire'. 'The Roundo' was the old name for the Globe Theatre in Southwark where William Shakespeare's plays were performed. In Aberdeen, William Black & Co of Devanha Brewery, Ferryhill called their East India Pale Ale 'Roundo'. Polmuir was a hideout for Peter Young who tried to release prisoners from the Aberdeen Tolbooth. He was successful, whereupon they took to the hills and 'Red Beard's Cave' at Durris.

For lovely girls often meet new loves
you can go to the market
you can go to the fair;
you can go to the church
on Sunday and meet your love there
(An excerpt from a ballad, 'Young Molly')

The Theatre staff.

St. Nicholas Street, (1906)

Dr William Sinclair's carriage and house staff outside the family home in Golden Square. The gardens in the centre of the square were private.

O' a' the jobs that sweat the sark
Gie me a kintra doctor's wark
Ye ca' awa frae dawn till dark
Whate'er the weather be, O!

RUBISLAW TERRACE

From Rubislaw Place to Queen's Terrace

James Matthews, successful Aberdeen architect lived there, thus placing his seal of approval. If a sophisticated town planning scheme had been brought to pass, building of similar boulevard-type terraces would have spread further into the Lands of Rubislaw. James Skene of Rubislaw lived next door to Sir Walter Scott in Edinburgh, hence the use of names such as Albyn, Waverley and Abbotsford in Aberdeen, thus marking the Scott connection.

The crater of Rubislaw was created by the Gibb family. Until the quarry was two hundred feet deep, horse-drawn carts carried stone to the surface by way of a winding road. By the time it finally closed in 1971 it was four hundred feet deep, and a testament to the successful granite industry of Aberdeen and environs, which in 1912 employed approximately 1700 men including stonecutters.

Rubislaw Terrace from The Gardens in Albyn Place. Photograph by George Washington Wilson.

ST. ANDREW STREET
From Loch Street to Woolmanhill

This was the scene of the destruction of Andrew Moir's Anatomy Theatre, 19 December 1831. A dog had devoured some of the human remains that had been buried in a shallow pit. 'The yells and cries of the populace at the sight of the bodies was most appalling', and some fifty of them battered down the walls with logs of timber; en route to a hideout in St. Nicholas churchyard the worthy Mr Moir, who actually completed some valuable research, was ignominiously pelted with dead hens.

ST. NICHOLAS STREET
From Union Street to George Street

This street now stops short at Correction Wynd because of the St. Nicholas Centre. 'Little Woolies', the threepenny and sixpenny department store opened here in 1919.

The bronze figure of Queen Victoria stood on the corner from 1893–1964. Many courting couples met at 'The Queen'. The 'muckle steen wifie' was taken inside the Townhouse, away from the ravages of the weather five years earlier.

ST. PAUL STREET
From Gallowgate to Loch Street

This street dates back to 1842, and is partially laid out on the site of 'The Vennel', an overcrowded quarter which was itself widened in 1805. The Congregational Chapel, designed by Provost Matthews and St. Paul's School were flanked by the factory of Farquhar & Gill's colourworks. Paint, enamel, varnish, oil burners and refiners, hairlime and glass merchants; they became renowned for Bon Accord Enamels (marine paint).

Gray's School of Art and The Aberdeen Art Gallery. The gates to Robert Gordon's College are by Starkie Gardner of London who was famed for his hammered ironwork at The National Gallery, House of Lords and The Bank of England.

ST. SWITHIN STREET
From Queen's Cross to Ashley Road

Morgan's Buildings of 1895 rate as one of the most sophisticated tenements of its day. The street was better known for George Washington Wilson's photographic Works which backed on to his Queen's Cross residence.

Baron Corvo had discussions with Wilson concerning submarine photography, but was not taken seriously by the firm.

The 'Middlewalk' leads to the Auld Hoose which served as Robert Gordon's Hospital 1732–1882. The statue of Major General Charles Gordon, 1833–85, who died at Khartoum is prominent in the picture. The year before he died he said, 'I have done my best for the honour of our country.'

SCHOOLHILL
From Back Wynd to Rosemount Viaduct

Originally known as the Schoolhill Wynd. Above Reid & Pearson's Corner where the brae of today's Schoolhill meets Back Wynd, there stood The Song School, another ancient foundation was the Grammar School, the earliest reference to which is 1262, when Thomas de Bennum was described as 'Rector Scholarum de Abirdene'. Perhaps the most famous scholar here was Lord Byron, whose sports included kite-flying, boating and swimming. The boys of Robert Gordon's Hospital used to be known as 'Sillerton skytes'. The derivation of this term has been the subject of discussion, namely that the founder was originally 'of Silverton by Aucterless.' There was a farm on the north side of the college named Sillyward which also provided a clue. The school uniform comprised of a tailed coat of blue cloth which was cut short, having yellow cuffs and facings, corduroy knee breeches and waistcoat with full gilt brass buttons.

Robert Gordon never married, and applied his parsimonial principles even to himself. He made no secret of it that he made his gloves last longer by carrying them in his hand; however his trustees buried him in style, giving the reason that 'it was too late for Mr. Gordon to object'.

The Old Grammar School (1757). In  1880, there was a scheme to lease these severely plain surroundings as a museum and art gallery. Gray's School was built in its place.

SEAFIELD

'The name of a dwelling a half a mile south from Rubislaw and the bleachfield'.

SHOE LANE

From West North Street to Queen Street

The name commemorates the work of the Shoemaker craft. In the nineteenth century Shoe Lane had 'a foul and narrow mouth that belches odour into Broad Street'. Whether this was 'The Street of a thousand smells' is now a matter for conjecture, but 'pails were put out for those who had a piggie'. Mr West Digges had a modest theatre which later became a stable.

SHORE LANE

From Regent Quay to Virginia Street

This street was known as Custom House Lane in 1809.

The shore porters' impressive warehouse with corner turret, altered the appearance of the street, which was susceptible to flooding from spring tides, in 1897.

SHUTTLE LANE

From East North Street to Park Street

This street was originally approached through an entrance arch dated 1828. 'Battered moleskin trousers hung out on poles, and some of the folk that bade here used jute bags as shakedowns.' This byeway is not to be confused with Shuttle Street (off John Street).

> There wis a mannie an' a wifie,
> and they were corkin' bottlies;
> says the mannie tae the wifie:
> keekle cackle cocklies.

SILVER STREET (NORTH)

From Golden Square to Skene Terrace

This street was laid out over the Longlands c.1820.

SIM'S SQUARE

From Blackfriars Street to John Street

Sim's Square was named after James Sim (1853).

SKENE SQUARE

From Gilcomston Steps to Caroline Place

An old turnpike road, once flanked by pantiled cottages, where one sink on the stairs served several households. John 'Spanish' Phillip's birthplace near Gilcomston Steps was a humble abode. When he died aged fifty, he had become renowned as the best colourist of his day. On the declivity known as Steps of Gilcomston there was a large boulder known as one of 'The Stones of Gilcom', 'A huge mass of close-grained granite, some eight feet high, being three-and-a-half feet broad and two feet thick; the outline being rather irregular'. When Alexander Smith wrote in 1882, it had been broken up. On the other side of Skene Square apprentice shoemakers lived and worked in the 'Rotten Holes', a long range of tumbledown sheds of one storey. They had to upturn their wooden brosebowls to prevent fouling overnight. Horn spoons were kept free of industrial and atmospheric grit. They slept on narrow bunks filled with straw, and laid down their weary heads on leather aprons that needed a sheen of hair oil to soften them.

☞ Cinema House, Skene Terrace.

SKENE STREET

From Black's Buildings to Skene Place and Whitehouse Street

Divided by Rosemount Viaduct into Big Skene Street and Little Skene Street. At the top of Little Skene Street stood the library fountain, and at the foot of the street, in part of what formerly was 'a four neukit garden' designed by the artist Jamesone, there stands reconstituted, the Old Well of Spa. Stone seats surrounded 'The choice medicinall spring; very specifick for grout, gravell, collick and hydropsie'.

The spring water is also lost to the city.

> If food was scarce, some bairns would
> take it upon themselves to sing for
> their suppers round the 'backies'.
> These back yards have since been
> removed as part of a plan to bring
> back a rural air to The Upper
> Denburn. (The Lower Denburn runs
> from Poynernook to Spa Street.)

The Central School replaced a row of Georgian houses. Dominating the view is East United Free Kirk, now ☞ Simpsons.

SKENE STREET (WEST)

From Whitehouse Street to Victoria Street

James Matthews was the architect for The Aberdeen Grammar School, and chose the Scottish Baronial style. Despite additions to the original design over the course of a century, the silhouette remains architecturally articulate. The original Grammar School portico from Schoolhill serves a useful purpose as a corridor link in the grounds. Prior to the statue of it's famous pupil Lord Byron by Pittendreigh MacGillivray being erected at the front door, the Denburn formed a natural 'Ha'. Today with the rolling lawns and mature trees it is amazing to relate what massive engineering feats were accomplished in order to culvert the Denburn and bring about the embankment of Esslemont Avenue.

Facing the Grammar School is the now converted Melville Kirk, by Brown & Watt, 1903. The final stages of the tower are based on the companile of St. Mark's at Venice. Unlike the internal arrangements of that building, the kirk's auditorium was arranged in the shape of a horse shoe. The link with Venice doesn't stop there however! Frederick Rolfe, better known by his literary title of Baron Corvo, lodged in Skene Street. He was thrown out in his pyjamas for non-payment of rent, and ended up in Venice as a gondolier.

Cherryvale lay in a coppice of fine trees, approached by a drive. J. L. Dickie, whose family entertained Jenny Lind the singer there, writes that the old house preceded the more renowned 'Castle'. During its construction, Mr Dickie built a thirty-foot wall in order to maintain his privacy.

A Riddle

Come a riddle, come a riddle, come a rot-tot-tot;
a wee wee mannie in a reid reid coat—
a stave in his han' an' a stone in his throat;
Come a riddle, come a riddle, come a rot-tot-tot.
(The Cherry)

Dr William Barclay, who wrote a very learned tract in 1615 upon the curative powers of the Well of Spa waters commented that 'barbarous apothecaries, Highland leeches, mercurial mediciners and all those who could give no reason for their calling', gathered here. One of the inscriptions on the well went missing. It read:

The stomach reins the liver spleen yea sure, 'a thousand evils' this wholesome spring
   doth cure.

  'Cherryvale', Skene Street (West).

Skene Street 'Backies'.

Skene Square

The Rotten Holes at Gilcomston Steps. On the right is Rodger's Brig, the access to John Street. A tannery stood on the other side of the burn. Gratings were placed in the burn in 1811 to prevent children from falling in. Today, Rotten Holes has become a car park, the tannery has disappeared, and a new brig spans a railway cutting.

SKENE TERRACE
From Skene Street to Summer Street

The first ever photograph of the moon was taken here by George Washington Wilson in December 1865. He collaborated with David Gill, an astronomer.

In contrast to all this experimentation, 'Sowens Jean' made sowens for customers who used to get them three times a week Sowens are made with the flour of oatmeal that 'lurks' in the inner husks ('sids') of the oat grain. (See 'With a Fine Feeling for Food' by Janet Murray the North East authoress.)

Craigwell Place ran from Skene Terrace to Skene Street prior to the Rosemount Viaduct being built.

Come, citizens of Bon-Accord,
An' members of the council board,
To you I'll spin a line or twa,
About our ancient Well of Spa.

Oor civic rulers weel hae deen,
For they an active part hae taen,
In gettin' richt oor ancient springs,
Oor brigs an' burns, an' ither things,
Sae Aiberdonians ye may blaw,
Aboot yer' ancient Well o' Spa.

SPA STREET
From Skene Square Bridge to Woolmanhill

A hundred and twenty years ago houses here were approached by bridges over the West-burn. The Garden Neuk Close was nearby, but the most well-known building was the Spa Bar.

SPRING GARDEN
From George Street to Windy Wynd

The name is a London one, and Spring Garden near Trafalgar Square is a good West End address. William McKinnon, whose factory dominates the Aberdeen street, laid high-quality castings. Their work, alongside that of the Aberdeen Adamant Paving stones made the finishing touches to the Granite City.

The Well of Spa in its original position, complete with surmounting gas lamp, and steps.

131

Mid Stocket Road

STOCKET FOREST LANDS

By the eighteenth century, the old Stocket Forest was little else than stone, whins and bracken. It formed one of the seven Royal Forests of Aberdeenshire. Beechgrove Kirk (1900), by Brown & Watt with its Te Deum window by the artist and etcher John M. Aiken is the 'Cathedral of The Stocket'. The South Stocket Road has been renamed Kings Gate. Honey Brae Farm, adjacent to nurseries latterly, made way for bungalows. An old man could actually point out the room where Lord Byron spent a summer holiday. His associations with this quarter of the enlarged city have been perpetuated with the name Byron Square in Northfield. The poet wrote: 'and so our life exhales—(a little breath)—Love—Wine—Ambition—Fame—Fighting—Devotion—Dust—. . . perhaps a name.' Did he get his priorities right in Aberdeen? For many years there was a well-known 'Lovers' Seat' in the Stocket.

STANLEY STREET

From Albyn Grove to St. Swithin Street

The feuar who laid out this street in 1876 had family connections with exploring, so named it after Henry M. Stanley.

STEVENSON STREET

From Leadside Road to Upper Denburn

This street was laid out before the South Mount Street viaduct was constructed. The extension act of 1883 destroyed at once the appearance of the street and its use as the Denburn to Rosemount interchange. William S. Stevenson was a tea merchant who carried on his business in Belmont Street.

STIRLING STREET

From Hadden St. to Guild St.

The Imperial Hotel was the venue for one of the highlights of the social scene, namely the Aberdeen Magical Society Annual Dinner. Guests were wined and dined right royally, then entertained to a feast of magic.

SUGARHOUSE LANE

From Regent Quay to Virginia Street

There was mention of paving in this street in 1824. The old Sugarhouse was where cones of sugar were stored.

The Sugarhouse is not unique to Aberdeen, and can be found in other Scottish ports.

SUMMER STREET

From Union Street to Skene Street

Derives its name from the pastoral-sounding Summer's Croft.

 Looking up Summer Street.

SWINE'S CLOSE

From the foot of Jack's Brae to Skene Street

Some unofficial historians say that this short cut was named after the local piggeries. These were croftlands, and as the name of Hardweird implies, soil was unyielding, and consequently from ancient times pigs were kept in the district.

There can be no dispute now because Swine's Close has been renamed Skene Lane. The Town's 'ground officer visited a royalty stone here as he conducted officials around the inner city boundaries when they checked to see that none of the "March Steens" had been moved'.

TANNERIE STREET

From Schoolhill to Loch Street

This street, which became known as George Street in 1824, was laid out in 1764 on ground west of the Tannage Yard.

THEATRE LANE

From Regent Quay to Virginia Street

By the lamplight, lonely, gleaming—
by the corner of the lane,
stands a lovely, lonely maiden—
'come, who will buy my pretty flowers?'.

The match and flower girls stood by the back door of the theatre, and sold their wares to performers. Then moved stance to the front door of the 'Old Bandbox' in Marischal Street. They saw Paganini arrive at the changing rooms to give a concert. The deep impression 'his wax-coloured face, long streaming hair, and the mysterious expression

Burning of North of Scotland Distillery, Aberdeen, 27th Sept., 1904
Damage £106,000, including 700,000 gallons of whisky.

his eyes made', followed his audience home.

The Kemble family converted a house fronting on to Marischal Street into the city's principal theatre, (1795–1873). It could seat six hundred, and the boxes near the roof were known as the Sweep's Boxes. William 'Sink—'em' Smith provided good founds for the adjoining houses, which had stable facilities in the basements with access into Theatre Lane.

THOMSON STREET

From Rosemount Place to Loanhead Place and Victoria Park

John Morgan, one of the city's most important master masons lived here at number 57.

The North of Scotland Distillery buildings in Union Glen were taken over by Messrs Harper Motor Company. There was a spectacular fire here on 27 September 1904.

UNION GLEN

From Springbank Terrace to Cuparstone Row

If it were still the day of the horse in the city, this place would be a massive stable. Instead it is turned over to motor cars and light industry.

A few cottages survive behind the Holburn Street frontages, but they postdate, 'Cuparstone' the Clachan of the wooden cupmakers.

The last water-driven mill in Aberdeen was Lower Justice Mill, and the site was cleared in 1931.

UNION GROVE
From Holburn Street to Forest Avenue

Famous for its front parlours replete with pianoforte. It was at number 42, that James McBey pulled his first copperplate etching (a simple study of Point Law loons) on the laundry mangle, when he was working at the George Street branch of the North of Scotland Bank (see John Street photograph).

Union Grove mansion and its landscaped grounds were planned to be yet another city park.

The Misses Duncan's Boarding and Day School for Young Ladies was housed here, until it was decided to build Union Grove over the grounds and dam that supplied the Upper Justice Mill. Cromwell Road is the extension of Union Grove. The name was selected because he was considered a 'safe personality'; during the years 1651–60 justice was impartially administered. The bastion that was built at Castlehill during this time was constructed of stone taken from the Bishop's Palace in Old Aberdeen.

Union Grove looking towards Holburn Street.

St. Nicholas, Union Grove by architects Ellis & Wilson. Its style has been described as 'Italian Renaissance of a severe type'. It was converted into flats in 1979. Union Grove Buildings opposite (1887), is by Matthews & Mackenzie.

UNION ROW
From Union Street to Summer Street

This was one of the Rows of the New Town, and there were no shops. Amid the houses were carriage building workshops and later car showrooms. *The Bon Accord*, a journal with a high standard of editorial had its headquarters here.

Horse-drawn double deck tramcars were built here by R. & J. Shinnie for Aberdeen District Tramway, one is now in the Museum of Transport, Edinburgh. An office block called Grampian House has now usurped the place of the carriage company, but in the annals of the history of transport this place is not forgotten, as landaus were supplied as far afield as London.

George Abel wrote: 'The cheenge fae horse an' kerriage gars me irk: a foumart o' a motor gyangin' fuddrin' to the toon, to the station an' the kirk.'

UNION STREET
'From Castlegate to Bawbie Law'

The sound of harness, and the voices of ostlers could be heard, as William Bain who was strapper to the Defiance coach, hurriedly prepared the carriages for their departure. This traffic, and the bustle of people thronging the street on summer evenings further delayed the horse trams on their single track, when the eighty-strong, fourth Aberdeen Artillery, Volunteer Citizen company, wearing dark green uniform, marched from gun practice at the Beach Battery. They were dismissed in the gas-lit stable yard behind the massive water house. The cistern contained 94,728 gallons, the value of which in 'fire water' at 4d. per gill was £50,521. Supposing it were porter, it would take a man five years and 127 days to empty, measuring off 200 pots per day. Today the premises have been converted into a bank.

When the snow set in, private sleighs with bells were brought out. Bakers' vans were mounted on runners, and goods traffic required the aid of tracer horses. The tramcar company used rough wooden horsedrawn sledges that carried twenty people; at stopping places, those in the back were in danger of being shot off.

Bon-Accord Street

Summer Street corner and the northern side of Union Street seen from Union Place which was numbered differently until 1889. In the foreground is the Free Gilcomston Kirk, which with the Langstane Kirk are the only two sandstone buildings in Union Street.

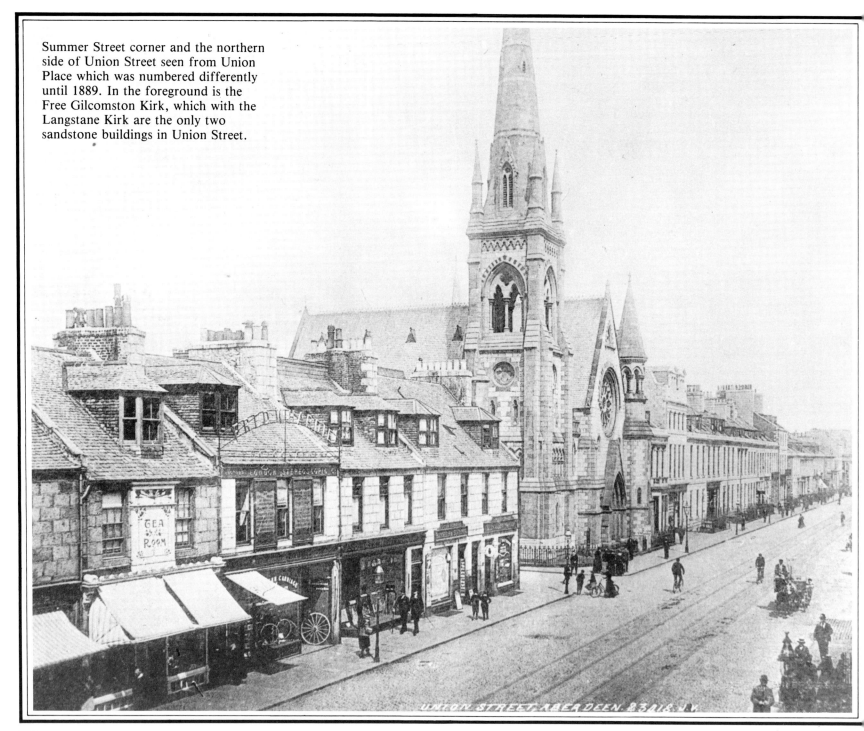

Pratt & Keith's Building, later The Palace Hotel which was run by the Great North of Scotland Railway. Complete with a Moorish-looking lift, and 'cleaned warmed air circulated by Blackman's fans'. Its billiard room was hung with gold and leather papers and lit by a massive domed roof. The hotel enjoyed a covered private entrance from the station. ☞

An English excursionist, writing 'The Land we live in', remarked about the spacious rooms in his hotel near Union Bridge; having on arrival noticed the clean brass doorplate and flowing muslin curtains at first floor windows. At table there was delicious bread, 'white as driven snow, and as light, with fresh butter worked into swans, Scottish lions and cupids'. Coachguards were at the hotel on the appointed hour, active and courteous in red coats and hats. Outside the colonnaded Royal Hotel and Posting House, portmanteaus and guncases blazing with crest or coronet, indicated a departure to the Highlands.

Visitors sometimes thought that the fisher-women's mutches were 'tall Flemish caps' and were interested to see their 'foreign looking ear-rings'.

Jewellers' shops shone in the sunlight; 'a perfect blaze of wealth and ornamental beauty.

249 Union Street.

The Townhouse being built, *c.*1867. Peddie & Kinnear the Edinburgh architects were accused of not knowing the nature, quality or value of granite as a building material.

Union Street celebrates the Union of Great Britain and Ireland which occurred in 1800, the same year as the Act for bridging the Denburn was passed. This is history, not matrimonials, however. Walkin' the Mat created a lasting bond between those who 'clicked' down the lover's lane of Union Street. As long as you had money for a café and a bus fare that was the only outlay you had to think about as the tram turned the corner of Holburn Junction or clanked to a halt at the Queen, on the corner of St. Nicholas Street. Maybe it was an illusive wisp of train smoke reaching for the stars beyond the Monkey House or the bright chalk of pavement pictures, that made their hearts strangely warm. Granny could not spoil the feeling of anticipation of young 'Northern lights' even if she tried throwing a candlestick if they arrived back home after ten, for often, wedding rings that were sold by weight were already chosen. Girls in service were similarly restricted by time on their evening out.

Queen Victoria affectionately referred to 'my neighbours of Aberdeen', and remembered one tradesman in particular; the hatter Samuel Martin, who advertised in doggerel verses. When he stood at his open window wearing a red Garibaldi shirt, as Her Majesty's coach passed by, she heard his name mentioned and said approvingly of this patriotic gentleman with the waxed moustache, 'That is the little hatter.'

The Mat was the southern pavement between the Athenaeum and Market Street; The Carpet was the section from Market Street to Bridge Street. Older onlookers were there to bide even if nobody was waiting for them at the Monkey House, Student's Corner, The Catwalk or The Queen.

'Jimmy Hay's Restaurant', wrote Eric Linklater in 1929, was 'black and gilded about the ceiling. The smoke of the richest reddest steak in Scotland had darkened its mouldings, and ghostly vineyard perfumes haunted every corner.'

Cabbies waited outside in groups smoking their short clay 'cheekwarmers' 'yarning of men and horses into the sma' hours'. Cabbie's harness polish was made of 'Black Beauty' boot polish, powdered resin and ordinary wax melted by the heat of a carriage lamp.

They kept the cold out with the hipflask, and sometimes had a solitary nip as they sat with a bearskin over their thighs, having thrown the leather rug over the horse.

King Edward's Statue, Union Terrace.

EDWARD VII
1841—1910

'A king in the making'; King Edward in the granite yard.

In 1935, the Majestic Cinema replaced the last of the Union Street terraces of dwelling houses with 'sunks' which were enclosed by ornamental railings. The architect T. Scott Sutherland also suggested replacing the trams with a new over-head type of silent electric vehicle from Switzerland, which operated by means of a magnesium strip below the road surface.

UNION TERRACE
From Union Street to Rosemount Viaduct

The terrace and gardens were laid out 1891–3, and the bronze statue by Bain Smith of Robert Burns contemplating 'the wee modest crimson-tipped flow'r' was unveiled on 15 September 1892. James Philip and Arthur Taylor sculpted the statue of King Edward VII which surmounts the 'Royal Loo' along with the 'Triumphs of Peace'. Guests at Mann's Grand (later Caledonian) Hotel, who had come north to Aberdeen from the capital could be forgiven if they awoke still thinking that they were overlooking Princes Street Gardens.

A few of the original Union Terrace properties survive, but the Old Free Bon Accord's chapel was the first to be put down for 'redevelopment'.

The Upper Denburn looking towards Woolmanhill. Garden Neuk Close, notorious for its overcrowded conditions was in this locality.

UPPER DENBURN
From Spa Street to Jack's Brae

This street has been truncated due to the building of the Denburn Health Centre with car park massif. All memories of the Denburn watersplash, Collie's Brig and the famous Spa Bar have gone in the march of clinical progress. The drey horses that used to come to Messrs Ironside's bottling plant adjacent to the South Mount Street Viaduct, would today lose their sense of direction.

The Upper Denburn looking towards Skene Street.

The bairns of the Upper Denburn played 'leavio', 'kick the cannie' and 'hoist the flag'. 'Barley Door' was their favourite, and they all stood in a row—one would stand in the middle, and the object was to try and reach the opposite side without being touched by 'the mannie in the middle'. The last one to be touched was the winner.

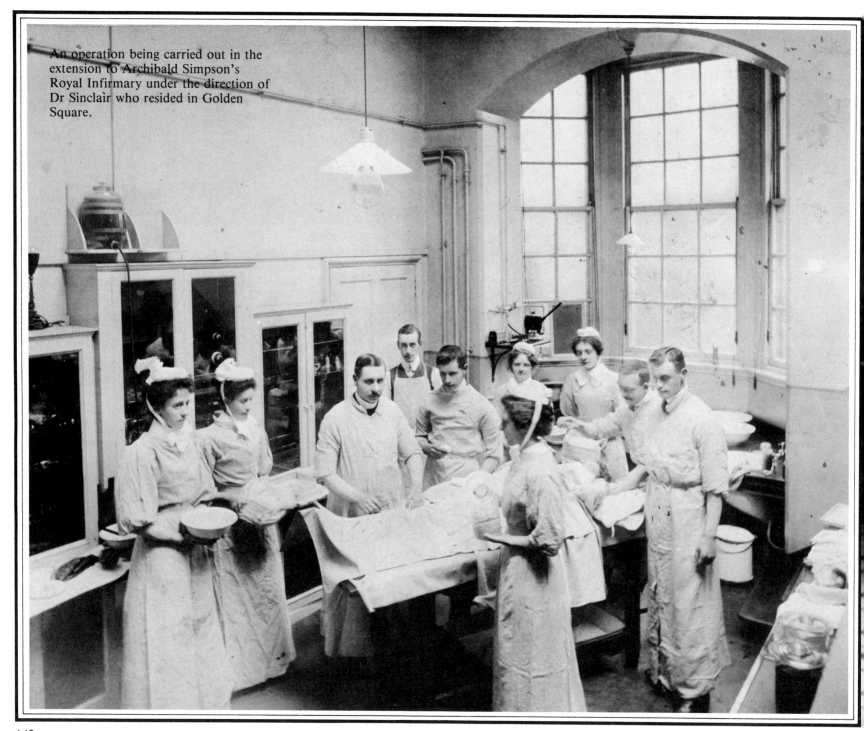

An operation being carried out in the
extension to Archibald Simpson's
Royal Infirmary under the direction of
Dr Sinclair who resided in Golden
Square.

'Cuninghar Hill' Hospital, called after the Broad Hill conies. The clock and bell (1766) were brought here from the Broad Street water house upon its demolition.

URQUHART ROAD
From King Street to Links Road

A tenement street, famous for its Hogmanay activities, and named after the first chairman of Aberdeen Land Association, Robert Urquhart. The first 'council houses' were erected in this vicinity in 1919.

In the summer, East End folk walked to the beach past 'sma' shoppies' that hung childrens' buckets and spades outside their doors. On the way, the Gordon Highlanders might be seen on parade at the Links.

Young pupils at King Street public school proudly made needlework samplers, demonstrated darns, and could 'turn a heel' well. All high quality workmanship—sad to relate, there was a high infant mortality rate, and nearby 'Cuningarhill' was built as a fever hospital. It is an ancient saying that if toonsfolk had a malady, they must be 'put to the Links'. During the plague years, many mass graves were dug there.

The first plague in Aberdeen occurred in 1401 due to poor crops and malnutrition, and the third and worst happened in 1647, when 1760 people died, one quarter of the population. All stray dogs were destroyed, all beggars were branded and anyone concealing the disease was 'puneist to the deid'. Three gibbets were erected to deal with any traveller so stricken, one at the Brig o' Dee, the Mercat Cross and the Haven mouth bore the other two.

Dr Bodie.

On a more cheerful note, the famous Dr Walford Bodie was born here. Hypnotist, cartooner, conjuror and ventriloquist, he claimed that the 'MD' stood for 'Merry Devil'.

'Yorkie' won the hearts of passers by with a performance of chanting and snatches on his mouth organ. A few bright pennies always covered the bottom of a New Year's biscuit tin that was his constant companion. 'Twang' was another local celebrity.

VICTORIA STREET
From Albyn Place to Skene Street

Built in the days of the young Queen, Archibald Simpson's terrace is simplicity in granite design. James Scott Skinner resided here, and played his stroch violin to the delight of those who admired his fiery brilliance. The granite trade considered that many a good tune is played on an old fiddle, so extra care was taken with 'the grain of the granite' on the 'Strathspey King's memorial'.

VIRGINIA STREET
From Weigh-house Square to Commerce Street

The slopes below Castlegate were congested with buildings until 1978. St. Clement's Manse with its postern gate, approached up a flight of stairs was the chief architectural loss along the path of the Inner City Link Road.

The cry of 'Send out your fighting men' no longer echoes around the bonded warehouses, and the banjo players, 'Ingin Johnnies' and accordion players can no longer be found by visiting seamen.

Aberdeen Pynours or Warkmen, otherwise known as the shore porters were selected for their great bodily strength. They were familiar figures with their 'decent black dress suits and braid bonnet'. Sedan chair bearing was their monopoly. The last person to use a sedan chair to and from her town residence was Mrs Allardyce of Dunnottar.

The Bowie Well and Bannerman's Bridge 1768–1982 are other vanished landmarks of Virginia Street. Sculptors William and Alexander Brodie were born here, and even Byron lodged here for a short time.

The north side of Virginia Street looking towards Castle Terrace. St. Clement's Manse can be seen in the foreground.

McWilliam's Workforce in Virginia Street. James Street was approached through an archway adjacent to the snug bar.

Wallfield House, Rosemount, (now ☞ Wallfield Crescent and Place).

WALES STREET

From Park Street to the Tarry Briggie and Victoria Place

This street paired with Albion (England) Street. G. M. Fraser considered the possibility that it could have been named after an Aberdeen artist James Wales. At one time it was known as Well Street. There was a flesh-market as well as a cinema known as the Casino here. Little Wales Street linked Wales Street to Hanover Street.

WAPPING STREET

From Trinity Street to Lower Denburn (Now removed)

Probably named after old fashioned fishermen's garb, but there are other Wappings in England and Scotland which are associated with the ancient craft of boat warping.

Wapping Street contained the first gas office. Nearby were wood-merchants' yards where the first circular saw driven by horse was introduced to Aberdeen.

WATER LANE

From Regent Quay to Virginia Street

This street was one of the Shorelands' slums. The floors were made of brick and hard-baked earth, and the walls were mildewed. One old woman who was lucky enough to have had garret accommodation during the floods told the inspector what she had witnessed: 'Bless yer sowl aye . . . it wis an awfu' time. The fowk doon the stairie wis near-droonit wi' the water comin' in upo' them.'

WELLINGTON PLACE

From Union Place to South Bridge

The south bridge is still in existence, and crosses over the Howe burn. Union Place has become Union Street, and Wellington Place has transferred its locale to a road joining South College and Crown Street; so now the great road south (Holburn Street) runs from Brig o' Dee to Union Street.

WESTBURN ROAD

From Hutcheon Street to Anderson Drive

Named after the burn of the 'weel-stocket' forest, which still flows in the open, through the remaining croft-lands of Silverhillock. Stepping stones, and fresh water cress, in the vicinity of the water splash, attracted bairns, who played in Sheepies Brae ('Bonny' muir and 'Hose' field, like the 'Cocket Hat', were all field names, so when darkness fell, only a glimmer of candlelight could be seen in the tiny windows of Ballgreen Cottage or Raeden Farm, up its shady 'Lovers' Lanie'.

The village of Loanhead lay on the other side of common pastures that provided grazing close to the granite quarry, on the stony ridge of Rosemount. This open tract of land was referred to as Glennie's Parks until the eighteen-

seventies, when the Civic 'Faithers' created Victoria Park.

The names of the mansions of Westburn yet remain, even though Westburn Park (1839), now in public ownership, and the pavilioned country seat of Woodhill House has been replaced (1975) by an office block which resembles a castle keep.

The original gas offices were re-erected on the corner of Mount Street, and in 1893 it was resolved that Mary Place, Mount Place, and Ann Place become known as Westburn Road.

WESTFIELD TERRACE

From Craigie Loanings to Whitehall Place

As topographer, Arthur Mee was accustomed to say, 'The daffodils were blooming when we called.' There is a commemorative garden here to the singer Mary Garden, who gave her name to the perfume, 'Gardenia'. During her retirement she played bridge in nearby Belgrave Terrace. Westfield Terrace's villas set in spacious grounds were the work of one architect, James Henderson.

WOOLMANHILL

From Schoolhill to Steps of Gilcomston

Schoolhill led to 'a little green swelling hill', properly known as the Woolmanhill. It was there that the sellers of wool gathered on market days up until the 1850s. The 'little round hill' described by one of the Duke of Cumberland's men, was St. John's Hill, which had the same dedication as the Dominican or 'Black' Friars. All of the houses in Woolmanhill were eighteenth or nineteenth century. Two famous historians were born here in 1809, John Hill Burton and Joseph Robertson. The latter wrote *The Book of Bon Accord*. The jumbled matter makes enjoyable reading, for it is infused with a keen, quiet, pawky sense of humour.

Within the first infirmary building (1742) there were 'four low cells for lunatics, fatuous or furious; others wandered about at their own sweet will'.

YORK STREET

'From Wellington Street to the north side of the ship building yards'

Two shipyards once occupied the entire length of York Street. Although Hall & Co, and Hall Russell & Co were neighbours, and similar in name, they were independent of each other.

Handcarts trundled heavy items from the blacksmiths' shop across the cobbled street to the yards.

York Street is named after the Duke of York, but not the one that had ten thousand men who he marched up to the top of the hill and marched them down again. The names of York and Clarence are meant to complement each other and they are not far apart. Charles Mitchell, born in 1820, was articled to an engineering firm in Footdee before he moved to Newcastle in 1842 after graduating at Marischal College. He became a partner in the firm of William Armstrong Mitchell and Company and made a fortune in building battleships for navies including Russia and was honoured by The Tsar for his part in setting up the first yard at St. Petersburg. His son, the artist Charles William Mitchell, carried out his father's wishes to complete the building work at Marischal College. The hall with its memorial stained glass windows, and the 235-foot tower are of 1895, and the family donated further monies towards the construction of the south façade.

YOUNG STREET

From Gallowgate to Loch Street

This street was opened in 1806, and named after Provost William Young of Sheddocksley.

'Whip ahin', yer horsie's blin'.' Loons had a free ride from Wordies' carters on their way back to the stables. A trail of granite dust was left along the kerbside down Denburn Road.

Waterloo Quay, looking towards Regent quay; The Harbour Board steam train coming into view. Waterloo Station, demolished in 1936, was the head offices of the Great North of Scotland Railway Company, and was the first passenger station that Aberdeen ever had in the City Centre (1856).

ABERDEEN
HARBOUR

POCRA QUAY
From York Street to North Pier

Anciently, street porters shouldered their 'pokes'.

A Fittie fisherwoman's song

We brak nae bried o' idelty
doon-bye in Fittie Square—
A' nicht oor men toil on the sea,
an' wives maun dae their share.

Sae fan the boats come laden in,
I tak' my fish tae toon,
an' comin' back wi' empty creel
tae bait the lines sit doon.

POINT LAW
East end of Albert Quay

Migrant fishworkers lived in tarry sheds there adjacent to their work. When they catered for themselves the salt herring was laid on top of the pot so that they could flavour the tatties. Three women in a 'crew' salted, gutted and packed the herring with the aid of a cooper. Fishing boats came alongside and discharged their crans, whereupon extra help from Torry filleters was enlisted by hoisting a flag they were ferried across the water. Before the River Dee was diverted, Point Law was part of the geographical area of Upper Torry. The inches, i.e. low-lying islands mid harbour, were Spillwater Inch and Midching e Inch.

PROVOST MATTHEWS' QUAY
A continuation of Blaikie's Quay

In 1885 a new quay was built, beginning at the south entrance to the dock, and extending round the point of the Inches and up the north side of the Albert Basin to the Graving Dock. It is a convenient wharf for 'passenger steamers', enabling them to enter and leave the harbour without delay. It had become the custom to name quays after the Provosts in whose time they were erected, and the new quay was called Provost Matthews' Quay.

'Ca' yer girds'.

Ellis & McHardy

In autumn, a schooner known as 'the aipple shippie' came into port with 'chippit' apples from the Channel Isles; small quantities of her cargo were fished out with a rusty 'dabber' and taken away in baskets, or even handkerchiefs. Sweet-tasting Spanish locust beans for cattlecake were shovelled into hoisting tubs with wooden spades, and children looked for them on the quayside.

REGENT QUAY
From Shore Brae to the Canal Basin

The original quay wall of unknown age, but pre-1400; was found near the Weigh House. The old Regent Bridge was replaced by a new and wider bridge which was opened and closed by electric power in 1905. That bridge and St. Clement Bridge have since been removed. Perhaps the most illustrious person to set sail from this quay was Peter Williamson who was kidnapped. He returned to Aberdeen and exposed his persecutors, then settled in Edinburgh and published the first city directory. The life he spent there during the thirty years that followed was said to have been more interesting than his adventures amongst the Hurons.

WEIGH-HOUSE SQUARE

The original weigh-house (or 'pack' house) was demolished in 1885 to make way for the Harbour Board offices, which are partially built over the hard stones which were utilised also by wandering showmen, cheapjacks, acrobats and street singers. Unclaimed merchandise was sold after a year and a day, but the purchaser had to surmise what was inside so this led to interesting speculation.

The outside gallery was built with material salvaged from an Amsterdam vessel which ran ashore on the Belhelvie sands. The walls were three feet thick.

The Weigh-house looking along Regent Quay towards Guild Street. Notice the railings which are there for the sole purpose of tethering horses. At the back of the square stood Bourtie's Bar.

'The Round House' Footdee.

Steam now to London twice a week,
thirty-six hours the time they seek
for the voyage to London Town,
and in the same time frae that come down.
Quick they run, they do not tarry,
goods and passengers they carry.
Twa steamboats, passengers, goods full,
sail for Newcastle and Hull.
Just once a week they make the trip
far quicker than a sailing ship.
Twa steamers weekly trade between
Dundee, Liverpool and Aberdeen.

(James Smith, 1892)

WATERLOO QUAY
From Regent Quay to York Place

Waterloo Quay wall was begun in 1811. The adjacent canal basin was on the north-west of the Lime Basin, both lying between the ends of Commerce Street and Canal Terrace. When Waterloo Quay was extended to its full length northward and joined to Regent Quay, the Lime Basin was cut off and rendered useless for ships. In 1834 the canal was connected to the harbour by a sea lock, and the following year the Lime Basin filled up, and afterwards built upon. The canal was given up to the Great North of Scotland Railway in 1853.

The booking office entrance to Waterloo Station; the wharf is adjacent, (right).

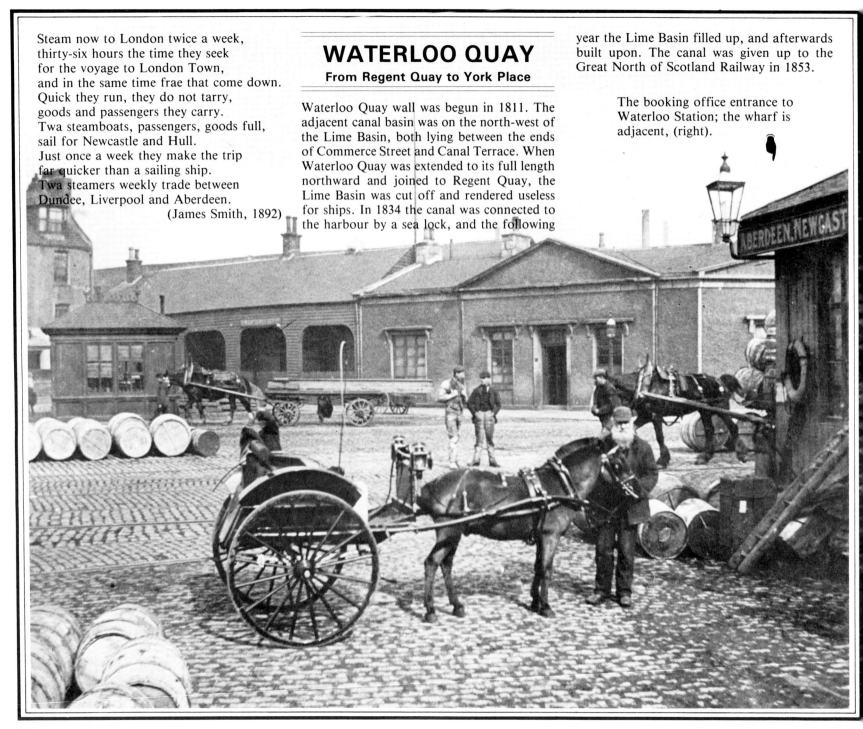

Street porters assembled for work five yards away from the edge of the wharf as prescribed at Waterloo quay, beside the London boatsheds, wearing Scotch caps and harness, more familiar to travellers in France and Belgium. They took back burdens of 1½ cwt and pushed weights of five hundredweight from the quayside up to Castlegate. Polished granite, bricks, ornamental cast iron boilers, agricultural instruments, chemicals, combs, woollens, winceys, tanned skins, carpets, candles, paper, pens, whisky, beer, brushes, rope, sails and provisions for victualling ships, a wide variety of exports for a city the size of Aberdeen in Victorian days, made this a busy port.

In 1848 Queen Victoria and Prince Albert visited Aberdeen, coming from London by sea, and the Royal Yacht was moored at the north end of Waterloo Quay where a triumphal wooden arch was erected. At this time there was not another dock in the British Empire where the Royal Yacht could have moored alongside a quay.

FOOTDEE

Alone by the dunes with the distant neighing of horses on the Queen's Links, before the Gasworks and seabathing station were built there was a smell of boilyards and boatbuilding. Incoming vessels might see a cow from the Shetland boat escape on arrival at Findlay's Buildings, and make for the north breakwater with 'chiels' and drovers in pursuit, past 'Scartie's Monument', a sewer vent. On 'the Back Links,' kitchen furniture was scrubbed down with sand on washday, when sheets were bleached, and clothes dried along the shore.

On Fridays, sandboys with their donkeys delivered fresh smelling sea sand for the floors.

Despite hard work, and up in the morning to 'teem breeks and gapin' leather', many fishermen were unable to raise the money to buy their cottages. Fittie men were well known as skippers with the herring fleet from Stornoway down to Yarmouth. At night, by the light of oily lamps the wives made nets to 'catch the silver darlings'.

If boats were in distress when crossing the bar, women tore their hair an clapped their hands; their piercing cries and frantic gestures could not be forgotten. A bust on the parapets of the pilot's office commemorates the wreck of a barque, the *Grace Darling*, lost offshore on 27th February 1874. Drink aboard the doomed vessel was significant, and there are no longer any public houses in the Squares, or on Pocra Quay, where men had their 'wacht o' ale' and lounged at the gable ends, or played 'pitch and toss', keeping warm by a particular sweeping motion of the arms.

Through the house, the 'guidwife at hame', welcomed unexpected visitors. 'It's sair matter that we're oot o' biskit an' fite breed: but there's ait kyaaks and bannocks t'ee.' Usually children were good eaters, having 'a crop fir a' corn, and a baggie to hud' it'.

Women sat on the seat by the Gents' 'Yettie'. wearing new wraps, white aprons and blue petticoats, and remarked about family likenesses during 'a Launchin'', when everybody got into the shipyards. Men who worked in the heat of the hulls at Halls', went home at night through the arch to Neptune Terrace, with their moleskins and linders so wet that they had to be left on the brass rail in front of the fire. On Fridays, the ganger was paid for piecework, and the money distributed in the Neptune Bar.

Fishing off Waterloo Quay.

ABBEY ROAD FISHER SQUARE

This is virtually all that is left of the traditionally built village of Old Torry, along with Wood Street and parts of Baxter Street. The square was the work of the architect who built Balmoral Castle. The 1870 gables of the houses faced the harbour, but the fisherfolks' front rooms looked out onto a courtyard. Many a quarrel broke out about whose day it was on the green.

BAXTER STREET
From Sinclair Road to Balnagask Road

This street was formerly known as Balnagask Road. The draw wells in this district add something to the local history: the Captain's Well was named after Captain Adamson, whose friend Captain Affleck gifted the ship to Nigg Parish church in 1829.

John Stephen's well near Abbey Road (at the back of Jubilee Buildings is also worthy of mention). There were wells in the policies of Balnagask House.

FERRY ROAD
From Sinclair Road to South Esplanade East

This now vanished street led to Jessie Petrie's Tavern which stood at the waterside before the deflection of the River Dee, 1869–73. In a plan of 1869, half the streets of Old Torry were down for removal following the Harbour Improvement Act. An osier bed and bleach-greens were another feature.

The Harbour, Aberdeen

156

TORRY

Prior to 1881, the village of Torry, Kincardineshire, comprised of the following streets: Ferry Road, Agent Street, Bank Street and School Road. In a century there have been substantial changes; the 3.6 acres of Old Torry being industrialised in 1974. At the turn of this century it became one of the most prosperous places in Aberdeen, and even yet retains a fierce identity of its own from 'fowk fae o'er the water'.

The villages of Burnbanks, Findon and Cowie and Doonies experienced an 'exodus' at this time, and the numbers were further swelled by English trawlermen and their families. Fisher folk from Collieston, Slains, Whinnyfold, Port Erroll and other small fishing villages also had their sights on Torry.

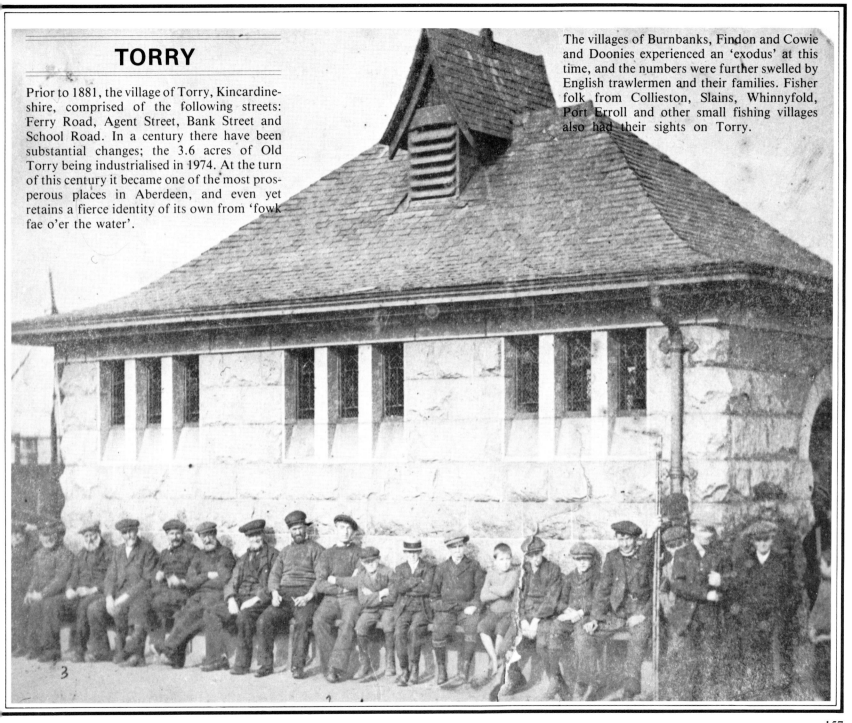

157

GRAMPIAN ROAD
From Victoria Road to Polwarth Road

This street is a reminder that Torry is built upon the foothills of the Grampian Mountain range. The street was extended in 1896, 'from Victoria Road on the east as far as to join Balnagask Road a short distance north east of Craiginches Farm.' The names of further mountains were decided upon when further building took place upon Torry Hill, namely 'Mormond,' 'Brimmond,' 'Morven' and 'Kerloch.' Many of the tenants are connected with the fishing industry, which has risen to such dimensions of recent years in Aberdeen.

GREENWELL ROAD

On the old road leading from Torry Farm House to Craiginches there was a well to be found on a green bank. The water from this well was piped down to the farmhouse, and the granite works near Victoria Bridge also took advantage of the water supply.

GREYHOPE ROAD
From Sinclair Road to Girdleness

This windswept road was named in 1893, although 'pebbles' had been bought for paving purposes ninety years previously from the quarry here and taken as ballast cargo to London by the Adam Brothers.

MANSEFIELD ROAD
From Sinclair Road to Balnagask Road

Originally this steep brae was known as Corbie Well Road. The well itself was at the junction of present-day Mansefield Road and Sinclair Road. A second well of the same name was dug at the junction of Mansefield Road and Abbey Road. The Derby Well was in the grounds of the old manse.

MENZIES ROAD
From Victoria Road to Grampian Place

This street was named after the Menzies family of Pitfodels who also owned ground on the south bank of the River Dee. The last of their line, John (1756–1843) bequeathed his property for a college where students could be trained for the Roman Catholic priesthood. The high part of Menzies Road overlooking the Wellington Suspension Bridge, is dominated by a long line of tenements with 'mansard' roofs. Torry Farm stood half a mile east of Wellington Suspension Bridge.

OSCAR PLACE
From Oscar Road to Grampian Circle

This brae commemorates the day of the whaling ship. A reminder that boats can be wrecked within sight of a great city. This was the fate of the *Oscar* at Greyhope Bay, Girdleness on 1 April 1813.

ST FITTICK'S ROAD
From Greyhope Road to Nigg Bay

This road was officially named in 1893. The Bay of Nigg was originally St. Fittick's Bay. The kirk was finally abandoned in 1829. There were numerous wells in the vicinity, and the first inn outside Torry on the coast was adjacent to the old kirk.

SINCLAIR ROAD
From Victoria Road to Greyhope Road

This street was named after David Sinclair of Loirston.

SINCLAIR ROW
From Sinclair Road to South Esplanade East

This formed part of the fishing village of Old Torry. The 'Torry Parliament' sat on a bench outside the public convenience nearby.

Old St. Fitticks

City from the south-west, *c.*1891. The Craiglug Rock is the focal point of the composition, with The Wellington Suspension Bridge which opened in 1831. The back road from the Millburn district of Ferryhill was another approach to the estates of Blairgowrie House and Arthurseat. Features of Polmuir included two conical hills over-run with heath and furze. The fir

'The Killees,' back of Mansefield Road.

tree plantation of Ewen's Woods with their cowslip covered banks was the work of John Ewen, Master of Arthurseat. Miss Duthie whose name is fêted in horticultural circles, succeeded him. The McGrigor Obelisk (Aberdeen's 300-ton answer to Cleopatra's Needle) which now stands in Duthie Park, was still at Marischal College quadrangle at the time this photo was taken.

Fa wid be a fisherman's wife
tae run wi' the scrubber an' the knife?
It's a doon-ruggin' life
an' it's up tae the mussels i' the mornin'.

Weel may the boatie row
that fills a heavy creel;
an' cleads us a' frae heid tae feet,
an' bus oor pottage meal.

'Fit'll we do wi' the herring's heid?
We'll mak' it into a loaf o' breid'.

"Men of Torry".
Left to right: Leiper's Dod, Sam Gray,
Cushnie and Mary's Joseph.
Kersey Cloth, "Fearnought" trousers,

First Trams from Torry, 1904.

Walker Road School.

Victoria Road.

SOUTH ESPLANADE WEST
From Victoria Road to Craig Place

In 1896, the embanking of the Esplanade left a considerable hollow between it and the houses in Menzies Road to be filled in with factories. All traces of Torry Farm have gone, along with another feature of the 'South Bank', James Ogilvie's boatyard. He lived behind the yard in Deebank Cottage. His fleet of 'boaties' numbered some four hundred. Orders included flat-bottomed boats for duck shooting from the Duke of Hamilton. The Ogilvies participated in the Dee swimming races, and were noted for their gallantry in saving lives.

The Northern Patent Brick & Tile company's brickworks were half a mile east of Torry Farm.

VICTORIA ROAD
From Victoria Bridge to St. Fittick's Road

An iron girder bridge was first mooted in 1877, but the strategic importance of this crossing point was fully appreciated and by 1881 the best of all 'The Royal Family' of bridges had been opened. Victoria Road was developed in the London 'mansions' style, but St. Peter's Episcopal Church (1898 benefactor the Laird of Cowie, Rev. Disney Innes) is the third 'Leading Light'. The view of it from Crombie Road prepares us for the impact to come, a rose window, high up in the gable end. The church may be incomplete, but its site is reminiscent of St. Bartholomew's, Ann Street, Brighton, one of the loftiest nineteenth-century churches in the world.

WALKER ROAD
From Victoria Road to Polwarth Road

The Aberdeen Land Association paid this compliment to James Walker, a local tea and wine merchant by so naming this street. (New) St. Fittick's church here (1899), by A. A. L. Mackinnon, is an unexpected study in the Romanesque style.

Torry Ferry

163

The Links from the Big Dipper.

The bathing station of the skyline was opened on 13 July 1898. The work of John Rust, City Architect. The warm hue of brick masonry harmonised with the green-toned roof. 'The Pottie' (Cannie Sweetpots) was formerly a regular bathing place for all those who preferred fresh water to sea water). 'Duckworth's Pond' was popular for boating. Both watering places have now been filled in and the baths demolished. The Bandstand, Trams, Boxing Booths, Pierrots and Professor Powsey with his balloon have all had their day.

Cattle from Shetland were herded off the boats into a large wooden shed by 'The Round House'. This distant view of the Fisher Squares shows scaffolding straddling the breakwater.

'For men must work and women must weep though the Harbour Bar be moaning'.

The Links during the First World War.

The European War, Aberdeen Links during the Crisis. Adelphi Series

An ancient rhyme for a game called 'beddies'. The lassies and laddies faced each other:

> There were three Dukes and a King of
>   Spain,
> who came to court Mary Jane—
> but Mary Jane is far too young
> to marry a man of twenty one—
> she bows to the east,
> and bows to the west,
> bows to the one that she loves best;
> when she comes to the one that's true,
> she'll turn and say, dear, 'I love you'
> But you're a' sae fat as barrels
> Sae upsy tupsy tee,
> o ye're a' sae fat as barrels
> Sae upsy tupsy tee—
> ye're a' sae thin as pokers
> Sae upsy tupsy tee.

SANDNESS

The point at which the New Pier originates was called the Sandness; near it stood the Blockhouse, which was subsequently used as a powder magazine. Further westwards was the Fisher's Boat Haven or Pockraw, at a considerable distance from Futtie Church. The Blockhouse, which has already been mentioned, was built to defend the harbour *c*.1477. Its walls were six feet thick, providing a good support for a chain to be stretched across the Haven in event of war.

The New Block Houe was built in the early sixteenth century on the foundations of the old one, the ground plan was semi-circular, or half moon shape; the embrasures pointing seawards, and had an arched roof which was considered to be shellproof. Nothing of this structure remains, its site occupied by a row of buildings erected in 1878.

Before breakfast, women shelled mussels or baited, and might walk in search for the latter as far as the Black Dog. Children who were late risers worked to the chastisement of 'Fat's keepin' ye, ye lazy quine.

South Pier Road, Footdee.

Seaton Pottery established in 1868 near the new Bridge of Don. John Gavin the proprietor kept the new Bridge of Don Hotel as well as making hand-thrown storage barrels for food, and personalised pottery gifts. The business was carried on after 1904 by others until Ivor Mills sold out to Aberdeen Corporation in 1966. High rise flats now occupy the site.

The future o' the toon to tell
Wid' maist need some prophetic spell
To rightly tell fit it may grow
As it does lapse of time pass through

But judgin' by the change I see
May hae some guess what it will be
So wishin' a'thing for it's gweed
It's people wark an' daily breid
A city be o' granite stone
Lang after I am deid an' gone.

(James Smith, 1892)

OLD ABERDEEN

BOATHOOSE BRAE

From Great Northern Road, over the Aberdeenshire Canal to the Aul'ton Market and College Bounds

This well-worn peat track was used as an approach from the west to Old Aberdeen, by the folk from Kittybrewster Cot-toun, who helped out at the 'hairst' when the surrounding fields yielded barley for the professor's private stills.

The Port Elphinstone flyboat berthed at the Boathouse (where the railway now runs), and on the day of the Aul'ton Market, folk made their way down to the cattle and horse fair. 'Bairns off school, held the working horses' bridles for saxpence.' Bargaining was slow and hard, snatches of conversation might be overheard, such as 'Foo much are ye needin' fer yer horsie?' (retort), 'Ah weel—gie me ten shillings.' As the buyer walked away, he heard the bridle being taken off by the other 'bodie', so knew that he would not have to give ten shillings for it.

During the war years, a complete yoke could cost £35. There was still a wide variety to chose from such as Argyllshire or Hielan' cobs, Clydesdales and hill horses as 'white as snow!' Your eye was your merchant and your foot your guide.' Two ancient fairs were held here annually as custom decreed. One, on the day before Good Friday was a cloth market known as the 'Skyre Thursday Fair', the other being the 'St. Luke's Horse market', held on 18 October.

The Aul'ton Horse Market. ☜

CHANONRY

**From the High Street, via Tillydrone Road
to Don Street**

The ancient layout of the Aul'ton Streets has been likened to a hangman's noose—the long High Street and a strangling circle of Don Street plus Chanonry. The symbolism doesn't stop with this disclosure, for the River Don is shaped like a shepherd's crook.

It took 200 years to build St. Machar's Cathedral, but it didn't last longer than thirty years without interference. In 1560, the tower was demolished, and 14 bells taken from the crossing tower. In 1688, whilst stone was being removed from the transepts for use at the fort on Castlehill, the crossing tower fell.

Katherine Trail, in her *Story of Old Aberdeen* mentions an interesting building that stood adjacent to the cathedral, namely the hospital founded by Gavin Dunbar, in 1531, for twelve poor men that 'were of good conversation'. It was described as having 'twelve little chambers with as many little chimneys for a little fire in each of them'.

Bishop Dunbar's Hospital.

The cathedral precincts were surrounded by a wall in which there were four gates. Cluny's Gate opened into the Chanonry and it was surmounted by an effigy of the virgin and the arms of Old Aberdeen, while an inscription upon it ran, 'Pass not this way unless you say, "Hail, Mary." By such a salutation you will obtain pardon.' The Laird of Cluny's house and garden, the most beautiful in the Aul'toun, were just inside it. Within these gates were the Bishop's palace with it's courtyard flanked with four corner towers, the manses of the Prebenaries, the convent of the Holy Sisters of St. Katherine, and Bishop Dunbar's Hospital for Men.

COLLEGE BOUNDS

From Spital to High Street

Students wearing tattered gowns bowed their heads in learned tomes as they passed by, ignoring horse and cart alike.

From a summer house on Hermitage Hill there was a fine view of the Aul'ton, and the three Powis mansions—set in their own policies—graced by mature trees.

After sunset, few folk would venture near a blocked-up gateway that still has the arms of Bishop Elphinstone set in the wall.

Bishop Gavin Dunbar added the spires of St. Machar's cathedral. They were designed to incorporate the triple crown or tiara of The Papal See. The great builder of the cathedral was Bishop Henry Lichtoun, and his name is perpetuated in the gatehouse building.

The Hermitage of Powis; a once familiar landmark of the Aul'ton.

The Hermit of Powis

The Hermit of Powis lived in his cell,
And shunned the converse of man;
His food was the coarsest, his drink was the
    brook
That near to the Hermitage ran.

The Snowkirk (St. Mary of the Snows) was dismantled in 1640, 'to repair decayed chamber windows and construct college yard dykes'. The University further ruled that the beadle of St. Machar's cathedral was not to open the ground until £8 for the privilege of interment was paid into the King's College coffers.

The rural aspect of the place is there for residents to remind them of the names of Orchard Lane, and Orchard Walk—beside the Firhill, near the 'Thickets' stood the 'Gibberie Wallie' where the gingerbread lady sold her morning bake. The Powis burn flowed swiftly past.

The minarets of Powis, are said to have been built as a mark of respect for Lord Byron's bid to free the Greeks from oppression. Cabbies, however, pointed silver topped whips in the direction of the ironwork, decorated with a crescent moon motif, and told tourists that Turks still lived there. To the bairns it was simply 'many towered Camelot'.

The Hermitage, which stood on a sand hill, was removed for its gravel deposits in 1926.

Bairns clambered along the high dykes or called to each other at either end of 'Powis' Whispering Wall'.

The starved corpse of Earl Leslie, dressed in 'hermit's claes', was found here,

(This saddening tale points out Stanley Robertson (an authority on Scottish balladry) has a better known precedent in the original version of 'Lord Gregory' otherwise known as 'Annie O' Lochiryan'.)

Both lordlings die of remorse, but the prophetic moral of the ballad comes from Mary Hay's father, who said that if his daughter, the 'Flower of The Don', became Earl Leslie's common-law wife, it would mean 'the winnin' an' the breakin' o' her hert'.

DON STREET
From High Street to Brig o' Balgownie

Thomas the Rhymer's Prophecy

The Brig o' Balgownie has sair waes to thole
Wi' a wife's ae son and a mare's ae foal
Down thou shalt fall, wi' a clash and a dird
A'tummel—rummel, flat wi' the yird!
When comes the time
ye'll find the Rhyme
As Thomas sayeth.

Looking towards the new Brig o' Don (1827–30) ☞

The Balgownie Bellringers. ☞

THE WINDING RIVER, BRIGS O' BALGOWNIE & DON, ABERDEEN

The Bede House was the home of Baillie William Logan and Janet Moir (1676). From the basement of this house at 18/21 Don Street led a passageway to St. Machar's cathedral. Seaton Cottages, further down Don Street were demolished in 1969, and Seaton House destroyed by fire six years previously. Some of James Gibb's work (1725) made this mansion a most distinguished building. There was a revival of racing in Seaton Park after the nineteenth-century meetings, the last being held in 1928.

HARROW ROAD
From Don Street to King Street

This street was named after John Harrow, who owned a croft there.

HIGH STREET

From College Bounds to St. Machar Drive

Cabbie Gray, at his stance outside the Town House, 'wore a black velvet jacket and shepherd tartan trousers.' He, and the shop keepers who stood at their doors when business matters didn't press, watched the brewery horses setting off to Balmoral on a two-day journey, laden with beer barrels for Queen Victoria's household.

Before the coopers went to work in the morning, they met in St. Machar's Bar for their breakfast of small beer. When the brewery closed, they sadly looked at the engraved lettering in the mirror that still confidently advertised an establishment that was larger in area than the original college itself. The sound of their hammers and those of the granite workers in the nearby yards often reverberated against the freestone walls of King's. Causewayers paved the Aul'ton Wynds, and were seen coming back to check their work on the Sabbath. Danger lurked in the closes such as Mackenzie Place and Thom's Court, when bairns played there, because heavy carts trundled past on their way to Donside Paper Mills, laden with pulp.

The name Wrights' and Coopers' Place is a reminder that salmon and salt fish required barrels to be made.

Meston walk nearby is named after William Meston, the poet who wrote 'In praise of The Renowned City', some time in the 1730s, pointing out quite correctly that,

For he who would this city's praise record,
of talent great must be, and deft of word . . .

O, brither man, hae mercy on 's, tho' sair
   against the grain
O, dinna brak' the Traveller's hert, that's
   unco like yer ain.
An' gie's a stance far we will hae the sun,
   an' win' an' sna,
An' maybe ye'll be nane the waur wi' Him
   'at lo'es us a'.

SCOTSTOWN MOOR

'The marisch or free moss of Perwinnes' as it is alternatively known. As the crow flies it is some three miles from the Royal Burgh. The burgh was absorbed by Aberdeen in 1891. From north to south it has a perimeter of approximately a mile; and from west to east a third of a mile average—some three hundred acres is virtually treeless. The botany of the moor has been more fully studied than has been the case with almost any other piece of ground of equal size in the neighbourhood of Aberdeen. Upon its sweet-smelling grass Belgian-bred horses grazed for a few days before the Aul'ton Horse Fair. One particular visit of the German gypsies was chronicled in 1906, when 65 trailers headed north to Aberdeen from Perth. Gypsies were recorded as being in Aberdeen as early as 1527; their chief occupation being palmistry. Scotstown moor was a comparable space to Mousehold Heath just outside Norwich, which was made famous by the oil paintings of John Crome, and the writings of George Borrow.

Mr McNab took this 'photie' of the German gypsies at Scotstown Moor, July 1906.

SPITAL
From King's Crescent to College Bounds

J. M. Bulloch wrote,

Gie me the grey howe at the fit o' The Spital
Brae
when the sun lifts up wi' a lowe fae the
wimplin' bay;
Gie me the blae howe on a winter's day.

When he wrote these words, I wonder if he had Boa Vista in mind? Behind Boa Vista were the 'Froghall plotties', considered to be an alternative university and to the south again, St. Margaret's Convent and chapel by Ninian Comper, whose craftsmanship can also be seen at St. Margaret's in the Gallowgate. His was the architecture of contemplation, and indeed the Spital has inspired some literary work despite the proximity of St. Peter's Cemetery with its granite angel and panoply of Death. The novelist George MacDonald had lodgings in a garret overlooking this place, which also had associations with lepers. Robert Burns' second cousin from Glenbervie, John Burness was buried in an unmarked grave here (1826) when he had perished amid a snowstorm near Portlethen whilst out book-canvassing. (Among other titles, one which had been highly rated by Burns himself as being the best ghost story in the language, was *Thrummy Cap* a legend of the Castle of Fiddes.)

TILLYDRONE ROAD
From Chanonry to Tillydrone

Heavy horses hauled the pulp carts up the steep brae, past the Motte. The giant slabs prevented wheels from sinking into the mud. Aul'ton men in search of a wager came to Seaton Park where horses raced.

College students played at the ancient sport of worrying the life out of the sacrists. This actually happened to one Downie, who expired after a mock trial and execution. The man's commemorative cairn originally stood at Berryden, but like the adjacent Wallace Tower, both are at Tillydrone today. An inscription reads, 'I cannot tell how the truth may be; I say the tale as t'was said to me.' Another 'claik', Peter Butter, the Aul'ton Tavern keeper, was given the treatment too, as this rhyme records:

They took a man, an' killed him deid,
an' stappit him in a holie;
Buttery Wullie, Buttery Wullie,
Buttery Wullie Coley.

WOODSIDE

A DESCRIPTION OF WOODSIDE IN 1894

'The atmosphere is charged with granite dust; factory stacks and quarry tips mingle incongruously with woods and pastures. From the Cruives to Stoneywood, the banks of Don are dotted with factories in all the stages between full activity and silent decay.'

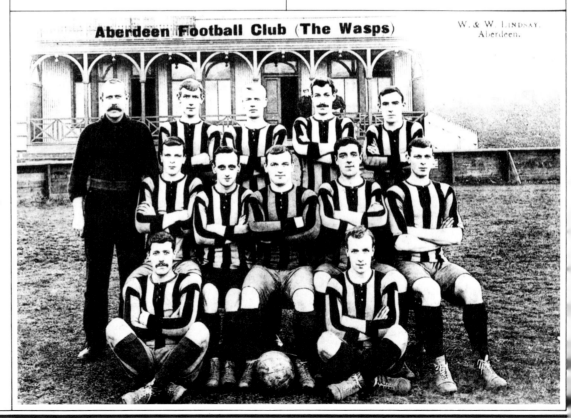

Aberdeen Football Club (The Wasps)

W. & W. Lindsay,
Aberdeen.

Old Aberdeen bar.

173

BACKHILL OF HILTON

A right of way for quarry workers working at Cairncry Quarries.

BANK STREET

From Great Northern Road to Gladstone Place

The Market Cross of Woodside stood at the top of Bank Street.

Mutter Howe High Street Old Aberdeen.

BARRON STREET

From Sandilands Drive to Great Northern Road

At Barron Street, the Port Elphinstone Canal was nearest the road at the station bridge. This street has been relocated, but was at one time one of the principal thoroughfares of the burgh; and named after Patrick Barron of Woodside House, 'Byron Hall'. At no. 177 was the home of Byron's nurse. John Anderson, 1814–86 who was in charge of the manufacturing of guns at Woolwich Arsenal spent his childhood at no. 19. He returned north however to give his library to his home town, (the Anderson Literary Association).

CLIFTON ROAD

From Powis Terrace and Great Northern Road to North Anderson Drive

This is the route of the old road to Inverurie. The first landmark is the Agricultural Hall at Cattofield where the quality of cattle bred for the colonies was a byeword 'of the civilised nationalities'. To the south-west lay 'Downies's Howe' where stood the memorial cairn to the sacrist, who died as the result of an unfortunate practical joke on the part of the university students.

The farm of Hillhead and the avenue leading to Hilton House (in addition to the broom, furze and hawthorn trees in the vicinity of Hilton Road) gave this area a rural aspect. Cummings Park also formed part of the Lands of Hilton.

Cotton Lodge, the home of Woodside's Provost stood in wooded policies, but the finest building in Clifton Road is the school of 1902 which looks as if it should have been placed instead on a seaside terrace. Specification details of the masonry work state that the façade is 'hammer-blocked; square-snecked ashlar grey granite with picked dressings'. It replaced 'Clarkie's Schoolie.'

CRUIVES OF DON

The 'Old Cruives' were originally a little below Persley Bridge which was built in 1891. There was a ferry at that point on the Don, and a boatsman's cottage. Following the demolition of the weir in 1664 by the Earl of Mar, the 'New Cruives' were erected a mile nearer Donmouth at a later date, and known as 'Rapahanna'.

Jimmy Coutts & Wife (water baillie c. 1930).

In the background is the linen, thread and cotton mill built in 1749. Gordon's Mills was run by Leys, Masson & Co.

DANCING CAIRNS QUARRY

A mile and a half outside Woodside on the North Road.

DANESTONE

In Monument Woods is a flat stone that was used as a writing table nine centuries ago by a Danish commander.

DEANSLOCH (Loch Goval)

Deansloch, otherwise known as the 'Bishop's Loch' is so named because on a small island there existed a summer palace and chapel belonging to the early bishops of Aberdeen. Corby Loch and Lily Loch are other stretches of water adjoining Grandhome.

The name 'Deansloch' has been applied to a residential district of Kettlehills and Northfield.

Strachan's bakery fleet at the Fountain, Woodside.

DEER ROAD
From Clifton Road to Gladstone Place

Named after the 'Dirra Dyke'. March stones 50 and 51 are at the top and foot of the brae.

DON STREET
From Great Northern Road to Grandholm

The famous Woodside Fountain was surmounted by a pillar lamp and was a general rendez-vous of meetings including the Salvation Army. Greig's Well was a 'weel-kent' Woodside name.

GRANDHOME

The Paton family gave the mansion house of Upper Grandhome its seventeenth-century appearance upon purchasing the property. It was originally a fortified tower overlooking the Don. 'Lower' Grandhome is spelt 'Grandholm' but a second mansion existed there at one time; vestiges of which have been incorporated as 'Grandholm Cottage'.

The north front of Grandhome House prior to the alterations of 1923. ☞

GRANDHOLM MILLS

In 1749, a company was formed to make cloth and linen at Gordon's Mills on the haugh of Grandholm. It was called Leys, Masson & Co. Mr. Paton, the landowner, granted permission to construct a canal a mile in length, to convey water from the Don to drive their machines. The first mill was seven stories high and had 386 windows. Over 3000 people were employed there until 1848 when the mills suddenly closed. Many of the workers found employment at Broadford's. Later on Grandholm Mills were taken over by J. & E. Crombie. Since then, the company has gone from strength to strength. There is hardly a country in the world that has not heard of Crombie cloth.

When Queen Victoria died, the courts of Europe ordered up vast quantities of dark cloth. These were indeed times of change, for when Jessie Fenwick from Tillycoultry brought with her the Galashiels custom of going to work in her coat and hat, women mill workers gradually ceased to be known as 'shawlies.'

Royal Aberdeenshire Highlanders, 1857; Major Paton is 3rd right. ☞

GREAT NORTHERN ROAD

From Powis Terrace and Clifton Road to Scatterburn

Originally, Woodside lay west of Deer Road; Printfield east of Deer Road, and Cotton, east of Don Street.

In 1894, Barron Street, Hadden Street and Wellington Street disappeared in order to become merged with Great Northern Road, which commenced with the Misses Riddell's Old Northern Hotel by James Souttar, the architect of the Salvation Army Citadel. One Geordie Turro squatted outside, on the triangular piece of waste ground. Upon the Laird of Woodside's querying his rights, he retorted, 'Deed, Lair', that's a question a gentleman widna speer, an' nae ither body has ony business. . . . '

The terminus for canal passengers to Port Elphinstone gave Great Northern Road some prestige in the eyes of country folk. There was a lock-keeper and superintendent of the Fly Boat House.

HAUDAGAIN INN AND SMITHY

Before the turnpike road was constructed, the old buildings were located where the lodge at the entrance to Woodside House now stands. There was a canal loch at this point. The name simply means 'a place where there is a fold', and the travelling people gathered on ground adjacent ot Haudagain shop in Great Northern Road.

Lord Byron heard this old ballad sung; and his poem 'So we'll go no more a rovin' (1817), was based on 'The Jolly Beggarman'.

There wis a jolly beggarman,
an' he was dressed in green,
an' he was seekin' lodgings
at a hoose near Aiberdeen.

I'll gang nae mair a-rovin',
late intae the nicht—
an' I'll gang nae mair a-rovin',
tho' the meenshine nae sae bricht.

The Little Wonder, a general store kept by the McKessock family in Great Northern Road. Andy McKessock was the authority on Woodside history, and made a cine film of the properties that were required for demolition occasioned by road widening.

HILTON

The name is derived from the menhir stone and two stone circles that looked out over the sea (Altein or 'the sacred firestone' at the mouth of the 'Black River'). Two stones of the south-west circle survived until 1871. The circles were contiguous to each other and were 30 yards in diameter.

JACOB'S LADDER

From Don Street to Grandholm Bridge

The old stairs were replaced in 1921; 1500 workers a day had used the old ascent, returning from Crombie's Mill to their homes in Tanfield, Cotton and Printfield.

LOGIE AVENUE

From Manor Avenue to Manor Drive

Francis Logie of Upper Middlefield gave his to a series of streets in this model housing scheme put up by the council.

MARQUIS ROAD

From Great Northern Road to Western Road

This street has no aristocratic connections, but nevertheless, is named after a lawyer.

PERSLEY DEN

'The castle' in Persley Den is known as the Barracks. In reality it was the purpose-built hostel for juvenile millworkers, or 'bound boys'.

WOODSIDE WORKS

The original Woodside Works covered an area of eight acres, where rags were broken down and sorted to degree of fineness, then cut into small pieces and shaken in a machine to free them from dust. Alex Pirie's Stoneywood Works continued the process of boiling and the making of fine writing and book paper. 'The Ragger's giant water wheel (130 hp) of 1826 was removed in 1967 to the Royal Scottish Museum.

In the vicinity of Woodside House stood a corn and snuff mill.

The staff of 'The Ragger', Woodside Works.

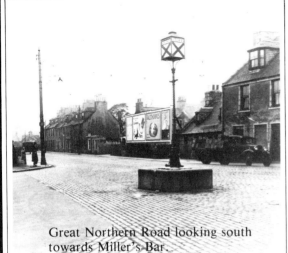

Great Northern Road looking south towards Miller's Bar.

The Meal Mill, Grandhome Estates. It was compulsory for all tenants to bring their grain to the miller and his wife who were given the special privilege of passing through Stoneywood Works to and from the ferry nearby.

Bucksburn Station

'Lousin' Time' at Grandholm Mill.

This picture of 'Jacob's Ladder is *c.*1897

PIRIE'S LANE

From Great Northern Road to Clifton Road

This street is named after William Pirie who was a woollens manufacturer at Gordon's Mills. He lived at Cotton Lodge, which stood nearby.

SANDILANDS DRIVE

From St. Machar Drive to Ferrier Gardens

The name of 'Sandilands' is big in Aberdeen, due to the Chemical Works employing a large workforce. It is also a bye-name for a man-made mountain pass of lean-looking tenements that stand four-square to the elements, in a manner so redolent of Aberdeen architecture.

The focal point of the housing scheme is Archibald Simpson's illuminated clocktower at the South Church (1845). It may not provide enough light to read by in bed, but it seems appropriate that the family motto of the Sandilands family of Cotton District reads, 'The Righteous shine as the stars.'

Place name associations here are particularly impressive. Sir David Ferrier FRS, who died in 1928, became an authority on the function of the brain. The last male heir of the Sandilands family had a high regard for the intelligence of dogs: A large number of canine friends kept him company during his last days. Other street names towards Tillydrone recall military men.

A Riddle
'Why did Tilly drone?'
(*Retort*) 'Because Kitty bruised her.'

(Kittybrewster and Tillydrone were at one time rival rural communities.)

The Woodside Postmaster and staff. ☞

SOCIETY LANE

From Great Northern Road to Clifton Road

Named after a yearly deposit society run by Messrs Robertson & Bisset in the sunk of the Laird's house. The 'thackit' cottages were known as 'Johnie Fee's Hooses'.

Child's Song
There was a mouse in a mill
rink-tum, billy-dilly ky-mee,
an' a froggie in a well . . .
Rink-tum billy dilly ky-mee:

Great Northern Road

STREET INDEX

which is dedicated to Berta McCrorie (Née Robertson); a true ambassador of Aberdeen

Map of Aberdeen
1920
Pages 185-196

Fonthill Road looking towards Whinhill Road, 1903.

184

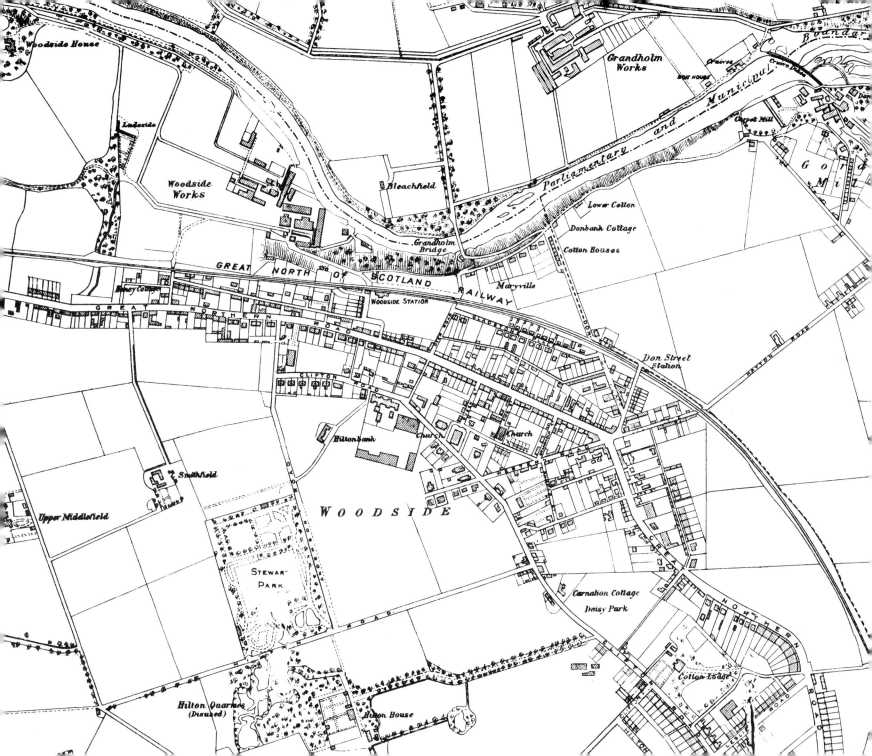

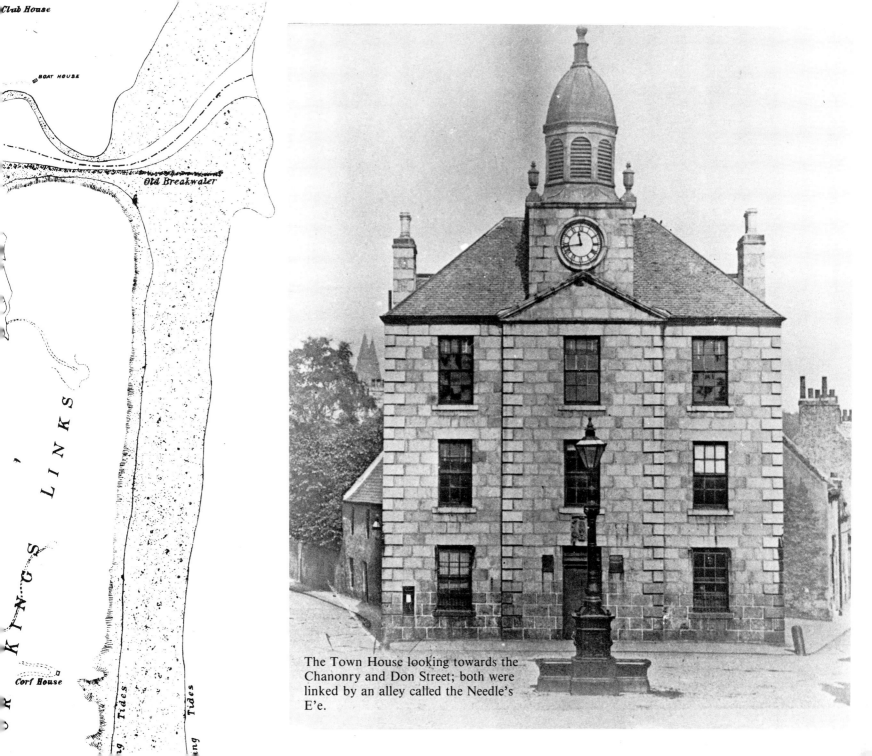

The Town House looking towards the Chanonry and Don Street; both were linked by an alley called the Needle's E'e.

Club House

BOAT HOUSE

Old Breakwater

KING'S LINKS

Corf House

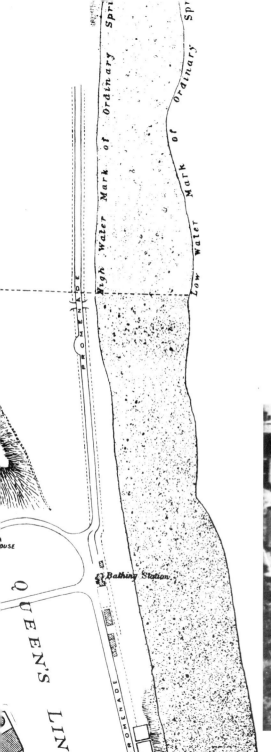

BON ACCORD

Gae name ilk toun, the four seas roun',
There's ane that bears the gree,
For routh o' mense an' grip o' sense—
It lies 'tween Don and Dee.

The Braif Toun, the Aul' Croun,
Time-battered though they be,
We'll cowe the loon, wad pluck them doun,
An' lan' him on the lea, lads,
We'll lan' him on the lea.

Sir William Geddes

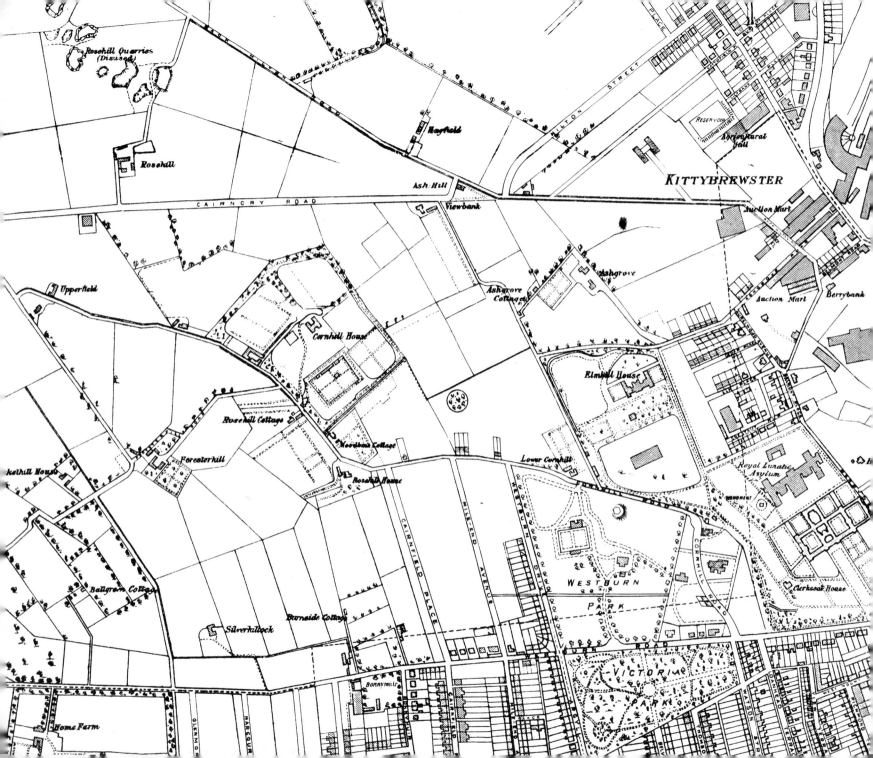

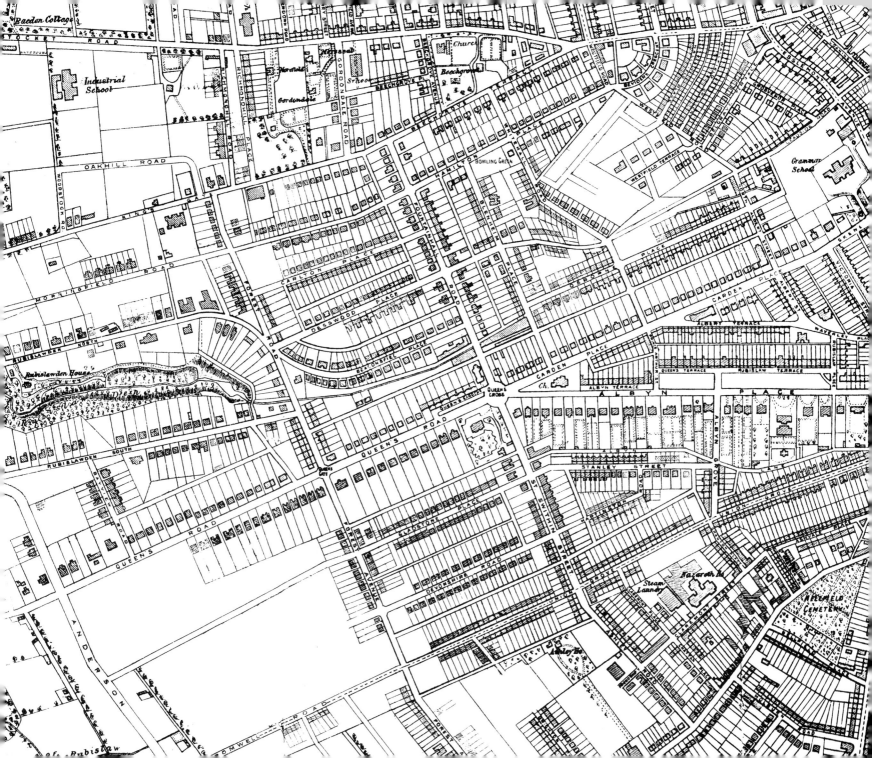

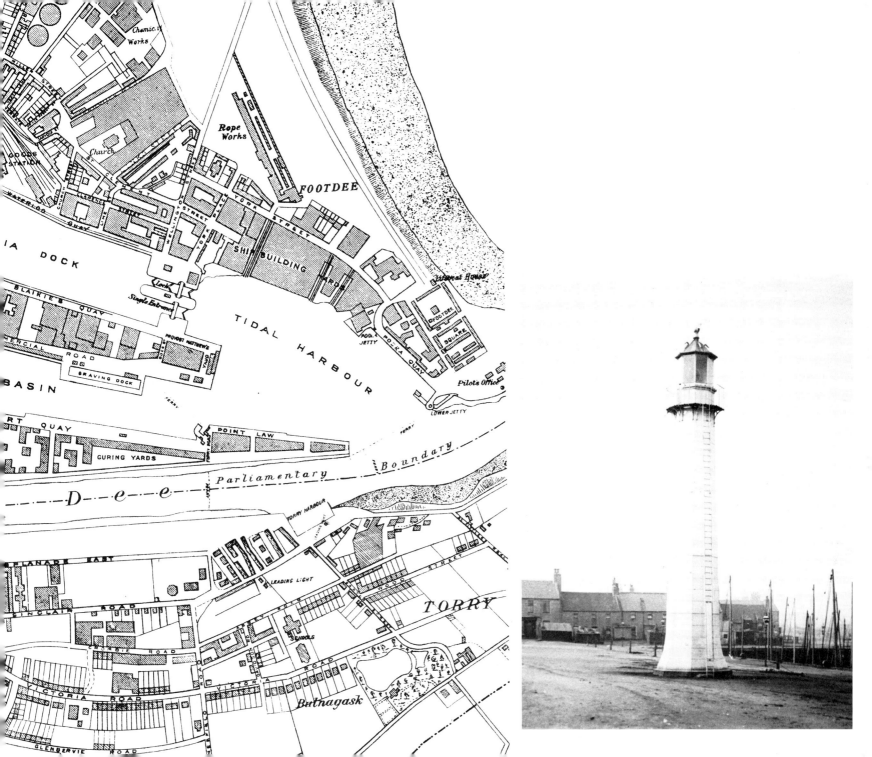

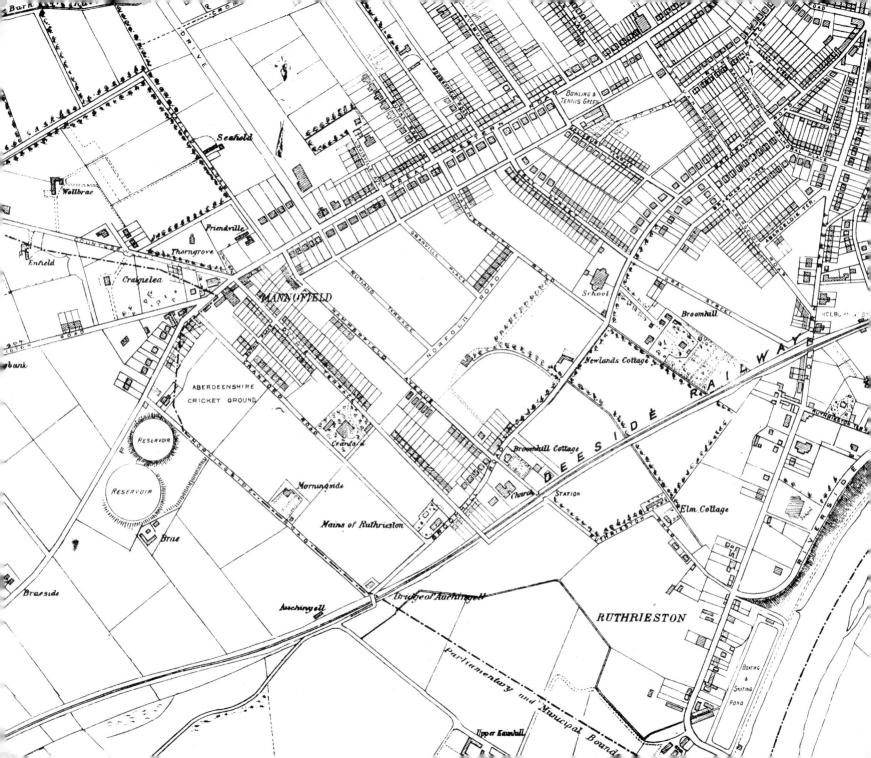

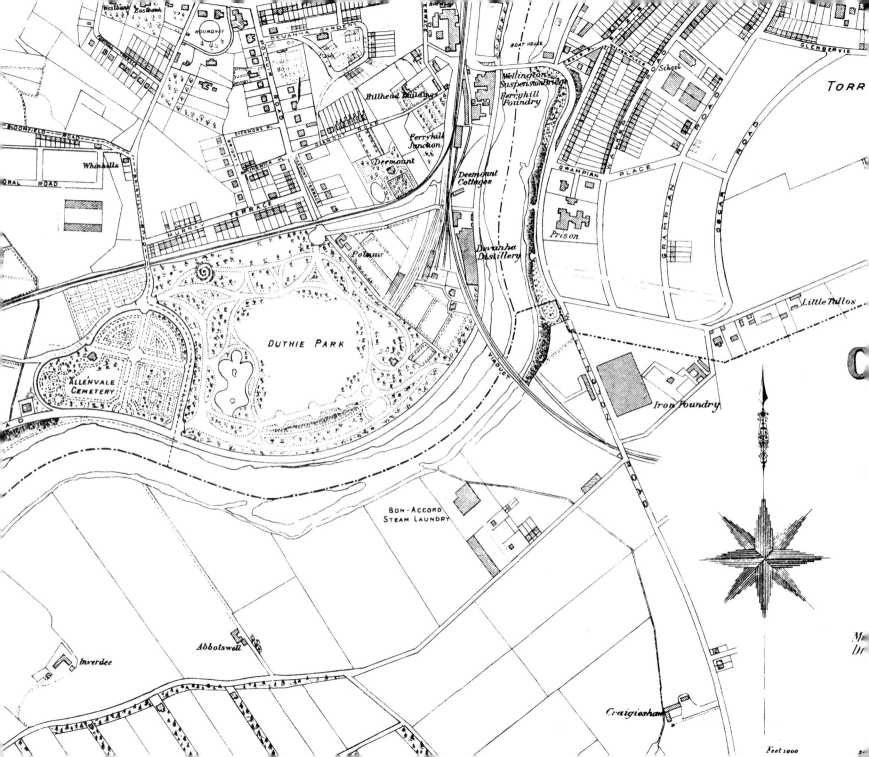

Westbank Eastbank

FOUNDRY

DEVANHA GARDENS

BOAT HOUSE

GLENBERVIE

TORR

Wellington
Suspension Bridge

Ferryhill
Foundry

Hillhead Buildings

BLOOMFIELD ROAD

Ferryhill
Junction

SYCAMORE PL.

School

GRAMPIAN PLACE

Whinhills

Deemount

Deemount
Cottages

ORAL ROAD

Prison

OSCAR ROAD

Devanha
Distillery

Little Tullos

MURRAY TERRACE

Potmur

DUTHIE PARK

VIADUCT

Iron Foundry

ALLENVALE
CEMETERY

C

BON-ACCORD
STEAM LAUNDRY

Inverdee

Abbotswell

Craigieshaw

Mi
Dr

Feet 1000

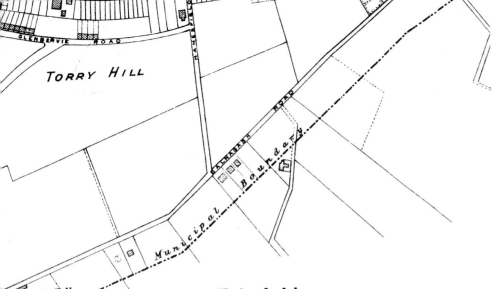

GLENBERVIE ROAD

TORRY HILL

Municipal Boundary

Little Tullos

PLAN
OF THE
CITY OF ABERDEEN
REVISED UP TO DATE
BY
G. CORNWALL & SONS,
MAP & PLAN LITHOGRAPHERS,
ABERDEEN.
1920

COPYRIGHT. ENTERED AT STATIONER'S HALL.

NOTES

Municipal & Parliamentary Boundary ,, ,, ——————
Division of Wards ,, ,, — — — — —

Scale $\frac{1}{7500}$ or 8.448 Inches to one Mile.

Feet 1000   500   0   1000   2000 Feet

The Tramway Tower Waggon at Ferryhill, 1903.